Dipankar Mukhopadhyay (b. 1950) is an alumnus of Presidency College, Calcutta. He joined the Indian Information Service and served in various media units of the central government. He was deputy director in the Directorate of Film Festivals and looked after the promotion of Indian cinema abroad. He also had a five-year stint as the managing director of the National Film Development Corporation (NFDC). After superannuation, he settled in Calcutta. He has two books in English and Bengali each on Mrinal Sen. He writes on various subjects including history, current affairs and the paranormal.

At Home With MRINAL SEN

Dipankar Mukhopadhyay

Om Books International

First published in 2024 by

Om Books International

Corporate & Editorial Office
A-12, Sector 64, Noida 201 301
Uttar Pradesh, India
Phone: +91 120 477 4100
Email: editorial@ombooks.com
Website: www.ombooksinternational.com

Sales Office
107, Ansari Road, Darya Ganj
New Delhi 110 002, India
Phone: +91 11 4000 9000
Email: sales@ombooks.com
Website: www.ombooks.com

Photographs courtesy of Kunal Sen

ISBN: 978-81-19750-25-2

Printed in India

10 9 8 7 6 5 4 3 2 1

To Subrata Sarkar,
A friend who is also a critic

Contents

Foreword

Another Time, Another World

Dhritiman Chaterji

My first encounter with Mrinal Sen ended with an admonition. This was in the mid-1960s. A group of us had managed to set up Delhi University's first film society and were trying to bring out a journal. This meant getting in touch with people like Sen, Satyajit Ray, Shyam Benegal and others through correspondence (read snail mail) and/or over the phone (which meant hanging around near a public phone booth and hoping that our 'trunk call' would come through in the next few hours).

We'd just had our first glimpse of the French New Wave courtesy the Alliance Francaise, had seen Sen's *Akash Kusum* (1965) soon after that. We couldn't help noticing a certain stylistic similarity which we interpreted as 'influence'. I sent him a questionnaire which included this question. He bristled, asking me not to try and 'show off' how much I knew. I recall that, even at the time, I thought he was being unduly sensitive. *Akash Kusum*, of course, became the Ultimate Duel to which Dipankar Mukhopadhyay devotes an entire chapter in his book *At Home with Mrinal Sen*. In the event, the journal never saw the light of day but it was my first contact with Ray and Sen. The rest, as they say, is history, even if I say so myself. But that's a story for another day.

Mukhopadhyay could be called Mrinal Sen's Boswell: *The Maverick Maestro* in 1993, *Kathapurush* in Bangla in 2003 (at about the time Sen made his last film *Aamar Bhuban*), *Sixty Years in Search of Cinema* in 2009 and now this book, which combines personal memories, a chronology of his films, an account, as I said before, of what Mukhopadhyay calls 'The Ultimate Duel' with Satyajit Ray and a long conversation chronicled over numerous sessions. Mukhopadhyay edits together these sessions into one seamless whole and renders the Bangla conversations in English without diminishing their spirit in the slightest way.

Taken together, this body of work provides a well-rounded view of the World of Mrinal Sen: his life, his worldview and, of course, his cinema, gleaned from what Mukhopadhyay calls their comradeship of four decades. I myself knew Sen and had lengthy chats with him (how could you not have 'addas' if you knew Mrinal-da!) over a long period of time. Even so, I was absorbed by Mukhopadhyay's recounting firstly because it unearthed events and insights I did not know about and also because my recollection of certain events varies a bit from his. It doesn't really matter whose memories are more accurate. The past, they say, is another country and it is not abnormal to lose one's way once in a while. What is important is that, in our own ways, we are able to take a deep dive, whenever we want to, into the world of a truly remarkable man.

Before I lose my way, let me recount an incident which illustrates perfectly Mrinal-da's fondness for adda. We were shooting *Aakaler Sandhane* (1980) and the unit was setting up a lengthy shot with lots of dialogue between Smita Patil (a brilliant actor, a wonderful person and a friend whom we lost prematurely and tragically) and me. Mrinal-da was, as usual, chatting with all and sundry. The shot was finally ready and he was ready to go. Smita and I protested that we had not been given any dialogue. His response was typical, in a way, of how he saw cinema. 'Oh, I've explained to you what happens in the shot. Now just improvise and we will be fine.' His cinema revelled in uncertainties, accidents and coincidences, leading to outcomes that were unexpected even to him.

During *Padatik* (1973), three days before shooting was meant to wrap, nobody knew, not even Mrinal-da himself, how the film would end. But end it did, with many people participating in the discussion. This, at least, is how I remember it. My memory of the incident may be a little different from the incident itself but is valuable nonetheless.

Maestro, Genius – Mukhopadhyay's deep admiration for the man is palpable. But he doesn't allow this admiration to lead to hagiography. There is no undue reverence here.

Both the recollections and the conversation are clear-eyed and objective. He asks the difficult questions and persists to exact the answers.

Who, then, is this book meant for? Needless to say, Mukhopadhyay did not write it with a particular audience in mind. He wanted to explore the life and times of a man who wore his greatness (although I hesitate to use the word) lightly for the sheer joy of discovery. It is meant for us, of course, who have some knowledge of Sen and his work. It helps enrich our understanding. Very importantly, it is meant for those who have an interest in the cinema, society and life of the 1960s to the 1980s but have no first-hand experience. It takes the younger generation much closer to those turbulent times. And therein, perhaps, lies its true worth.

1

Mrinal Sen As I Knew Him

The first time I was in the same space as Mrinal Sen, I had chosen to avoid him. It was in the lobby of a cinema hall in north Calcutta. The year was 1970 and the time was the Friday before the Durga Puja festivities. Among the pre-Puja releases that year was the film *Interview* directed by Mrinal Sen. Three of us—all students from Calcutta University, all gearing up to face job interviews ourselves—went to watch the film with casual curiosity. A year before we'd seen *Bhuvan Shome* and enjoyed it, but at that time what had made Mrinal Sen newsworthy and a familiar name was his legendary epistolary duel with Satyajit Ray. The two film-makers had gone back and forth on the pages of *The Statesman*, one of Calcutta's most prestigious newspapers of the time, arguing about antiquity and contemporaneity. Their arguments had started over Mrinal Sen's film about the middle class's desperate aspirations, *Akash Kusum*, released in 1965. By this time, Ray had established himself as one of Bengali cinema's most brilliant minds, and the fact that Mrinal Sen could engage in a debate like this made him stand out. How Bengalis love a good argument.

We were unprepared for the experience that was *Interview*. Starring Ranjit Mallick, who was then a newcomer, the film is about a young man trying to get to a job interview. What should have been a simple task turned into a portrait of a postcolonial city and a sharp critique of bourgeois, Eurocentric elitism. From the camerawork to techniques such as breaking the fourth wall, *Interview* shocked us, and it made evident Mrinal Sen's conviction that cinema was not just an artistic medium, but one that could potentially usher social change. *Interview* showed us the city we knew, stripped of romanticism and filtered through the lens of rage and cinematic realism. In one climactic scene, a desperate Mallick breaks a shop window and strips a suit-wearing mannequin. The violence of the scenc left us unsettled. Ultimately, he appears before the interview board, but instead of a suit, he wears a crisp dhoti and kurta. I won't tell you whether or not he gets the job. You can probably guess.

I still remember the silent file of young men walking out of the hall that afternoon. All of us looking confused, trying to figure out how we felt about the film we had just seen. As we made our way out, we noticed there was a man standing in the lobby of the cinema. He was tall, thin, dressed in a spotless white kurta and pyjama. His thick wavy hair was salt-and-pepper, he had long sideburns and he was wearing glasses with a thick, black frame. Everything about him suggested he was a left-leaning intellectual, an 'antel'. As people came out, he went up to them, asking what they'd thought of the film. I realized this was Mrinal

Sen himself, and I immediately charted a path that would ensure the film-maker didn't catch me. Aside from feeling too raw from the experience of watching the film, the bemused expressions of the people whom Mrinal Sen was pouncing on convinced me that wisdom lay in a swift exit. Once I'd gone past the danger zone, I surreptitiously looked back and saw a small group of people gathering around him. As we walked away, I heard him saying, 'You have every right to dislike my film, but give me a reason for that opinion.'

Not in my wildest dreams could the twenty-one-year-old me have imagined that there would come a time when Mrinal Sen would become Mrinal-da, that I would eagerly wait to spend hours discussing cinema with him, that the film-maker would ask me for my opinion on scripts that he'd written, and that I'd be able to tell him what (and why) I didn't like in the story he'd decided to narrate. His daunting six-foot-tall frame would become a fixture in my life. I'd get to know his family, and we'd become part of each other's worlds. He'd play with my daughter, who was strictly instructed to call him Mrinal-da rather than any variation of uncle. 'Just stick to Mrinal-da. All these kakas, jethus, mamas are very confusing,' he told her, speaking to the five-year-old like she was an adult. My daughter told him, 'You don't look like you're so stupid that you'll get confused. But okay, I'll call you Mrinal-da.'

I also vividly remember their first encounter. She was barely two and Mrinal-da, a sprightly fifty-nine.

Like many kids, she was making a fuss about drinking milk. Mrinal-da just took the bottle from her hand and regally announced, 'This is my milk. I am going to drink it now.' My daughter was a very silent kid. She did not cry or protest, only glowered at the intruder, fire and brimstone in her eyes. An undaunted Mrinal-da continued to talk with me while juggling the bottle. After a few minutes, she silently crawled towards his sofa with an uncertain smile, and Mrinal-da beamed at her and handed back the bottle. A sort of pact was silently signed.

My friendship with Mrinal-da happened thanks to my professional life. Almost ten years after the day I had first seen him, I was working with the Directorate of Film Festivals, and Mrinal Sen walked into my office at Lok Nayak Bhawan in Delhi. He wanted to cross-check the procedure for sending his most recent film to an international festival. The bureaucratic work was done in ten minutes, but the conversation flowed for hours. As a Calcutta youth who had grown up listening to conversations in the famous Coffee House of College Street, I was familiar with the fine art of the Bengali adda, but with Mrinal Sen it became an intellectual feat like nothing I'd experienced before. Over cups of tea—a staple fare of a government office—Mrinal Sen talked about cinema and Bengal's socio-cultural fabric, while making references to a dazzling array of international films. All my pending file work was pushed aside and forgotten. At 5.30 p.m., I made what at the time felt like an audacious suggestion on the part of a junior official who was speaking to an internationally acclaimed film-maker. Would he like to continue this adda at my home? I asked. I lived just three kilometres away, I assured him. Mrinal Sen agreed without hesitation. 'No problem, provided your place has some decent tea.'

By the time we reached my house, he'd become Mrinal-da to me, and I was just Dipankar to him. This was how we'd be with each other for the next fifty-two years.

That day, our conversation continued into the night. My wife Bandana walked in at 8 p.m. to find the two of us still talking, fuelled by cups of Darjeeling tea. Mrinal-da seemed a little uneasy at the sight of her, but before I could properly introduce her, he insisted on taking us out for dinner. 'Is there a restaurant we can go to in your hi-fi locality?' he asked. 'I generally don't have any money with me, but today I do, so I'm paying. But no high-brow place.' Bandana declined the offer, saying she had some urgent work piled up for the evening, so Mrinal-da and I went in search of a suitable place to continue the adda while we ate. We went to a modest dhaba-like eatery behind South Extension market, and as we sat on folding chairs on the pavement eating roti and chicken curry, Mrinal-da's master class on cinema continued. At about half-past midnight, the restaurant owner started washing the pavement. With a disgruntled expression, Mrinal-da stood up. Hailing a taxi, he said, 'This Delhi is not the city for a proper adda. Come to Calcutta, and we'll continue this session.'

As it turned out, we had some of our best addas not in Calcutta but in Delhi over the years, but I did take him up on his invitation when I next went to Calcutta, and visited his flat at Beltala Road. He introduced me to his wife, Gita Sen, who immediately became my boudi. I subsequently met his son and daughter-in-law Kunal and Nisha, respectively. Our friendship blossomed quickly. Soon enough I was almost a part of the family. We developed a pleasant intimacy, enjoyed each other's company—I could provoke him with my critical attitude. Mrinal-da defended himself with a rare indulgence. I say rare because that was how Gita Boudi used to describe our relationship.

The various film festivals offered me many occasions to spend days with Mrinal-da under one roof, when I could sit and chat with him and Gita Boudi without the constraint of time. During their visits to Delhi both of them also met Bandana, in her capacity as a programme producer with All India Radio, but curiously, they didn't seem to warm up to her much. This was unusual because few people can remain immune to my wife's charm. Yet Mrinal-da and Gita Boudi seemed distinctly disapproving. Mrinal-da possibly did not remember Bandana when he had met her in our house on his first visit. Later when he met Bandana it was as an interviewer for a radio programme.

Their paths occasionally crossed at press briefings and such events. But seeing Bandana and me at the parties that inevitably accompanied film festivals became a cause of concern for both Mrinal-da and Gita Boudi. They instantly recognized the easy intimacy between us, and the more they saw us together the more uncomfortable they became. When Mrinal-da met her during yet another interview session, he decided to impress upon her that it was important to make sure one's home was not neglected. Another day, during the same festival fortnight, Gita Boudi cornered me and told me to make sure I maintained a proper distance in my professional relationships.

That was when I realized I'd never actually introduced Bandana as my wife or mentioned I was married. Bandana wore sindoor and all the paraphernalia of a married Bengali woman so they knew she was married. We realized that Mrinal-da and Gita Boudi's disapproval of her and concern for me came from them thinking I was having an affair with somebody's wife! Bandana and I kept the ruse up for a while because it was just too much fun to watch the two of them misunderstand our relationship. When they finally cottoned on, both of them were visibly relieved and Bandana became part of our magic circle.

The relationship with Bandana was truly cemented, though, through a somewhat unexpected incident. A couple of years later, when Mrinal-da and Gita Boudi were in Delhi to attend the National Film Awards, Gita Boudi came to Bandana with a request. An invitation had been extended unexpectedly—could Bandana get two sets of Mrinal-da's white kurta and pyjama washed and ironed? Bandana said it was no problem and asked if she should buy a set instead since that may be more efficient than getting laundry and ironing done in the short time they had. The suggestion seemed to shock Gita Boudi. 'If you buy Mrinal clothes, this relationship will immediately end,' she said. Then she disclosed a little-known secret. 'You see, Mrinal has only three sets, and it's not by chance. We gave a lot of thought to what Mrinal should wear. In the early days, we could not afford money for clothes. So we decided that he would only wear simple white kurta and pyjama, and a black jacket in winter. That way, no one would ever know how many sets of clothes he had. For years, he's had only three sets. He wears one and the other two sets I keep washed and ironed, ready to be worn. He likes his clothes to be spotlessly clean. I've been trying to add three more sets. I think by next year I'll manage.' She then told Bandana not to speak of this conversation and 'Never try to give Mrinal any clothes. Ever,' she warned.

I'd always considered the simple elegance of Mrinal-da's trademark white kurta and pyjama as a sartorial choice. This conversation made me see the dignity he embodied and the idealistic passion that both of them shared. Both made difficult choices for the art to which they devoted their lives. After all, Gita Boudi had been an actress even before they had met, and in the early years of their marriage she would often take up small roles in films just to support Mrinal-da while he was trying to find his feet as a film director. They began their life in acute poverty because no one seemed to care for the socially conscious films that he wanted to make. But Gita Boudi understood his passion and commitment, and she made the choice to support him and make certain that he was not sucked into the world of commercial cinema in his desperate desire to make films.

Mrinal-da's only super-hit film was *Bhuvan Shome*, and that too was not by design.

Mrinal-da started his career as a film director with practically no financial support from any quarter. Neither he nor his wife had a regular income. All they had was their intense conviction that the films he wanted to make would be recognized as masterpieces. Even when that recognition came, it took a long time for their financial condition to change. For all the artistic richness that imbued their work, Mrinal-da and Gita Boudi lived much of their lives navigating poverty—so much so that Mrinal-da's entire wardrobe was three sets of white kurta and pyjama. Years later we would openly talk about Gita Boudi and Bandana's conversation, when Gita Boudi could laugh and say, 'He's got more than six now, but as it turns out, you really don't need more than three.'

Mrinal-da's small flat at Beltala Road, to which he had moved in around 1979-80, was an open house. There was always a stream of visitors—aspiring actors particularly from theatre, journalists, literary luminaries, politicians and people from his film fraternity. Conversation and cups of tea swirled endlessly in the small room where everyone was welcome. Mrinal-da never refused to meet anybody. The frequently overcrowded small sitting area was sparsely furnished and reflected the man, simple and spartan. A painting by M.F. Husain hung on one wall. It was a gift from the great master as a token of appreciation for the kind of films Mrinal-da made.

Mrinal-da had always been a workaholic, but in the 1970s and '80s he really had a lot of work, lots of offers to make films of his choice. This was a novel experience for both Mrinal-da and Gita Boudi. They discussed each film from the storyline to possible actors, went through the script in detail and agreed and disagreed on the treatment it required. Gita Boudi was always the first to read his scripts. But the script of *Chaalchitra* changed that equation a little and gave me a promotion of sorts. The year was 1981. In the previous year, Mrinal-da had made *Akaler Sandhaney*, which had received much critical acclaim. Energized by this response, Mrinal-da announced that his next film would be a tribute to Calcutta as he saw the city, his El Dorado, and would be called *Chaalchitra*. On one of my visits to Calcutta, he asked me to keep one evening free because he wanted to discuss the script with me. We sat in the Beltala Road flat, and he read out the script while narrating how he planned to shoot the film.

I listened carefully, but just could not share his enthusiasm. When I told him that the script lacked clarity, had too many loose ends and that I felt confused, Mrinal-da heard my points patiently, but I could see he didn't really care to listen and was also a little hurt. He didn't speak to me about the film again or invite me to the shoot when he started working on it. Eventually, *Chaalchitra* was completed and released in 1981 and failed to make a mark in the film festival circuit. The reviews were also not flattering. I got a call from Mrinal-da a couple of months after the release. He wanted me to repeat the points I'd raised about it when I had heard the script, and this time, he argued with me, defending his storytelling and treatment. But I could feel a subtle change in his attitude towards me. He wasn't just being polite. In our disagreement there was a measure of respect and on his part, a faith in my judgement.

A year later, I received yet another interesting request from Mrinal-da. At that time, I was still posted in Delhi. He wanted me to come to Calcutta as soon as possible because he wanted my opinion on a script he had just completed. No dates had been finalized for the shooting nor any actors approached, but there was an uncharacteristic urgency in his voice. I managed to organize some official work and landed up in Calcutta. When I showed up at Beltala Road, Mrinal-da looked sombre, but there was a suppressed excitement in his body language. He told Gita Boudi, 'I am going to discuss the new script with Dipankar, we are not to be disturbed, I will tell you all about it later.' Then he took me to their room, locked the door and read out the script of *Khandhar* to me.

It was based on a modern Bengali classic, *Telenapota Abishkar*, written by Premendra Mitra. The story was apparently very simple—about three busy city-dwellers who go to spend a weekend in a lazy hamlet and how their arrival creates hope and despair for the residents of the house they hire for the short getaway. I noted how Mrinal-da had maintained the pristine quality of the original story and yet transformed it totally. At the end of the narration, I burst out, 'Mrinal-da, this will probably be your best film.' He was elated, but it wasn't to hear praise that he'd called me. He went through the script with me again. This time we discussed different aspects, and I saw him jot down some of what I said in the margins.

Khandhar remains my favourite Sen film—*Kharij* is a close second—and my opinion was shared by many award juries. Beyond its subject and storytelling, what makes it special for me is that the film marks a critical moment in my relationship with Mrinal-da, when our bonds deepened.

This doesn't mean that we didn't have disagreements. Sometime later, on one of his visits to Delhi, he shared another film idea with me. This time I was unimpressed. 'Sorry Mrinal-da,' I told him after he described how he was contemplating the structure of the script. 'It just seems like a pale shadow of *Nayak*,' I said, referring to Ray's brilliant film exploring film stardom. Mrinal-da's response to my comment was a few moments of silence. Then he turned his attention to my young daughter. That evening, he left early, and I could feel the awkwardness between us. But the fact is no one ever heard about that film idea or the script. Mrinal-da quietly shelved the project. He didn't even attempt to make it. Another film that we never discussed was *Aamaar Bhuvan*, which ended up being his swan song. It is one of his most forgettable films. Mrinal-da and I always avoided speaking about it.

Looking back, it strikes me now that *Aamaar Bhuvan* was made at a time when Mrinal-da's world was changing drastically. Gita Boudi was in poor health, and although she had come out of an open heart surgery, it was clear that she needed to slow down. She had been his driving force for decades, and not having her by his side would unmoor him in ways that no one could have anticipated.

It's fitting that Mrinal-da respected my critical perspective because he played an enormous part in developing it. Not only did I learn from the conversations I had with him, but Mrinal-da always pushed me to deepen my understanding of cinema. For example, during the 1981 International Film Festival of India (IFFI), where Mrinal-da was a special guest of the festival management, he set up an interesting schedule for me. Every night, at around 11.30 p.m., he would call me over to his hotel suite. His opening salvo would always be, 'What films did you watch today?' This meant that no matter how busy my workday may have been, I had to make sure I'd watched at least one film so I would have something to discuss with him. Gita Boudi would join our adda for a while, but she would usually retire around 1 a.m. Mrinal-da and I would continue till 3 a.m. at least. The next morning, he'd come down by 9 a.m. for breakfast, all spruced up and ready to take on the day.

I've been fortunate enough to have years' worth of such conversations with Mrinal-da and other greats of Indian cinema. These sessions were my film school, and listening to people like Mrinal-da and actor Basanta Choudhury, another brilliant conversationalist, gave me incomparable perspectives into Bengali cinema in particular.

In 1994, I was unexpectedly transferred to Calcutta for a brief spell. Mrinal-da had recently completed *Antareen*, and his days were more relaxed. Sunday mornings at Beltala Road became a routine affair, and our adda continued, unimpeded by the streams of visitors. At that time, preparations were afoot for the centenary of cinema. Celebrations were being planned all over the country. Out of the blue, I got an offer from a leading publishing house to write Mrinal Sen's biography. It took me by surprise because I hadn't thought of myself as an author. Mrinal-da, on the other hand, had no doubt that I was the man for the job. He encouraged me to think about writing this book and assured me, without any hesitation, of his full cooperation. He offered unrestricted access to his papers, photographs, correspondence and most importantly, to himself. And so another facet was added to our relationship. I became Mrinal-da's official biographer. After finishing the first draft, I asked him if he wanted to read the manuscript. He declined and said he wanted to be the first reader of the published book. My attempt at framing Mrinal-da's life and work has received praise from many quarters, but for me what remains most special is how much he loved the book.

Our relationship was based on our shared love for cinema, but it was always beyond that. Mrinal-da welcomed me into his world, and he became a pillar in mine. When my wife and daughter had to stay in Calcutta alone—I was stationed in Delhi and tasked with a sensitive assignment that didn't give me time to visit Calcutta or spend any time with them—Mrinal-da would make sure they were comfortable in his favourite city. He would call them every night and talk about all and sundry including ghost stories. Those were never short calls, and Bandana remembers those conversations fondly.

My daughter remembers sifting through a pile of old photographs with him and discovering a picture of Mrinal-da in his early thirties. 'I was handsome, wasn't I?' he grinned and said, noticing her wide-eyed expression at the sight of his young self. Gita Boudi, who was also in the room, grinned and told him, 'Your looks were always the least important part of your personality.' With a twinkle in his eyes, Mrinal-da replied, 'Not at all. I always made sure people would notice me—when I entered a room, everyone would turn to see me. Remember my first white kurta and pyjama?' They exchanged a look and a smile, the shared intimacy of co-conspirators. It was a privilege to be allowed to witness these moments, though at that time, we may have taken it for granted.

Mrinal-da and Gita Boudi had become such a fixture in our lives that we never imagined that anything could change. But I was slowly coming face-to-face with a reality I had never wanted to face. I had never thought I would see the day when Mrinal-da wouldn't find the confidence to make a film. It happened with *Bhubaneswari*.

It was a storyline that had fascinated him for quite a while and had revived his interest in film-making. *Bhubaneswari* is a novel written by Bimal Kar. Mrinal-da once told me he had written and rewritten the script for *Bhubaneswari* four times. But I found he wasn't pursuing the project seriously. He often discussed the idea of making it and even talked to producers, but each time he took a step towards making the film, he would end up backtracking. At one point, his excuse was that he could not find the right face for the pivotal role of the old man in the story. In 2001, at a film festival in Pune, he met the legendary actor Dilip Kumar and excitedly told me that Kumar would be perfect for the pivotal role in *Bhubaneswari.* I reached out to Yusuf Sahab on Mrinal-da's behalf, and he immediately responded, saying it would be a privilege to work with Mrinal-da. Sadly, this time too Mrinal-da stepped back and the project never happened. He didn't even send the script to Dilip Kumar, and whenever I asked him about it, he would give me ridiculous excuses. Once, he said, 'Dipankar, the problem is Yusuf Sahab's wig!'

Around 2004, Mrinal-da and Gita Boudi shifted to a spacious apartment in Paddapukur (Kunal had bought it for them). Now Mrinal-da had a separate study-cum-office, but he no longer had the energy to work. He still wrote scripts, but most of them remained incomplete. I returned to Calcutta in 2010 after I retired from my government job. Mrinal-da was approaching his ninetieth birthday. While his body was unsteady, his mind remained as sharp as ever. Kunal and Nisha, citizens of USA by then, wanted to take them to live with them in their home in the States. But Mrinal-da and Gita Boudi flatly refused the offer. They wanted to stay in Calcutta among familiar faces.

Mrinal-da was slowly putting his years as a film director behind him. After a few visits it struck me that he no longer talked about making films or heard about what was happening in the world of cinema. Little by little, age caught up with Mrinal-da, and the dazzlingly brilliant man I'd known started to retreat. The most vocal and eloquent film-maker of his time gradually became strangely reticent. I had my own health challenges, but stayed in touch. At one point, I realized Mrinal-da was forgetting names, faces and commitments. He was conscious of his failing memory and retreated into a shell as these lapses became more frequent. The once-talkative Mrinal Sen emerged only now and then. On his birthday, surrounded by well-wishers, he would sometimes regain his old spirits. But those occasions were brief. He once ruefully said, 'We haven't had a real adda for a long time.'

A ritual that I developed was to visit him every year after Durga Puja, on the day after Bijoya Dashami. Bandana and I would take some rosogollas because it was his favourite Bengali sweet. He would hold my wife's hand warmly and smile at her, but the words were few and disjointed. One year, Bandana had worn a white sari with a yellow-and-red border. Mrinal-da touched the sari with fondness and said, 'You know, whenever I see yellow I can feel the smell of turmeric. My memory of my mother is associated with that smell. She used to cook and wipe her hands on her sari, which always had yellow patches and smelt of turmeric! Strange how these old associations can come back, isn't it?'

Mrinal-da's and Gita Boudi's health continued to deteriorate and slowly, they became first immobile and then bedridden. The stream of visitors was now a thin trickle. He felt embarrassed when any visitor came because he could not get up and greet them. Sometimes he could not even recognize the visitor but cleverly managed to hide his inadequacies. Dependant on their caregivers, the two spent their time lying in two beds, next to each other, their light dimmed. Talking required effort, and though Bandana and I visited them regularly, seeing them like that was heart-breaking. Mrinal-da mostly spoke about his time in Faridpur while Boudi would often remember their years of struggle, especially when Kunal was a child. For Mrinal-da, the worst blow was Gita Boudi's passing away. 'Gita has gone,' he told Bandana, holding her hands. Then letting Bandana's hands go, he said in a sad voice, a vacant expression in his eyes, 'She will never come back.' My wife couldn't find any words to say in reply.

The small group of caregivers who stayed with Mrinal-da told me that on some days, when he was well enough, he entertained them with anecdotes from his film-making days and even did jovial impersonations of politicians. He never complained about anything, but one of the nurses once found a piece of paper on which Mrinal-da had scribbled just one line: 'How are you? Are you okay? I am not.'

My last meeting with Mrinal-da was after Durga Puja in 2018. That day, he didn't say anything to me, but he grabbed my arm with all the strength he could muster and looked straight into my eyes. I can't explain that moment, but the gaze seared through my being and the expression in his eyes still haunts me. A few months later, the inevitable happened. My friend and mentor of over four decades left me on 30 December 2018. As his beloved city glittered in preparation for a new year, an inimitable part of Calcutta's beating heart stopped when Mrinal Sen breathed his last.

Mrinal-da, the self-proclaimed 'private Marxist', had no time for conversations about souls and the afterlife, yet once he had confided in me that in his early life, he had been a practising medium and had often tried to communicate with his younger sister, who had accidentally drowned in a pond. On a sombre and depressing new year's day, as I hobbled behind the cortege on his last journey, I found myself hoping that he and Gita Boudi had found each other again, and that I would also find him when my time came. He owes me an adda, and I'll have my answers ready to that familiar question, 'What films did you watch?'

2

The Films

If you had met Mrinal-da, within minutes you'd have noticed he had an impish sense of humour and that there was a tenderness in him, especially when he spoke to people he cared about. Yet these attributes are nowhere present in his films, which are grim and serious. Many critics feel that Mrinal Sen's films reflect an India that may seem dated in certain details, but still feels contemporary. Perhaps the warts of our society are more constant than the beauty.

To Mrinal Sen, film was not a medium of entertainment, but an instrument of social change. It was a vocation that he took not just passionately, but also seriously. Committed to making films that explored social issues, he consciously dismissed opportunities to garner popularity or attain box-office success. Never tempted by money or glamour, Mrinal-da remained true to himself and his convictions, and his films are testimony of this. In a career spanning about five decades, Mrinal-da made only twenty-eight films. It's a body of work that has explored middle-class India over time and held a mirror to both its resilience and its uglier aspects. For five decades, he made portraits of the urban middle class, with its various depravations, inconsistencies, contradictions and hypocrisies; dissecting action, thoughts and dilemmas mercilessly. It was a world he was familiar with. This journey started in 1955 with *Raat Bhore*.

Raat Bhore (1955)

Whenever Mrinal-da spoke to me about his first film, he said with characteristic candour that it was totally forgettable. He also described it as 'ugly' and 'uncouth', which I can't comment on because I haven't seen the film. However, my wife, at the age of five, did see the film when it released in theatres. From the vantage point of her mother's lap, Bandana's sharpest memories are of disgruntled faces in the audience, especially as they came out after the film. All I can tell you is that *Raat Bhore* had a spectacular cast—Bengal's matinee idol Uttam Kumar, Sabitri Chatterjee as heroine, veterans such as Chhabi Biswas, Chhaya Debi and Jahar Roy. By his own admission, Mrinal-da was unsure about what he wanted to do with this cast and the plot. At the time, he knew he wanted to make something that was unconventional, but the debutant film-maker also wanted to make a film that the audience would enjoy. However, that was not to be. *Raat Bhore* had a swift and silent burial soon after its release. Incidentally, the film released two months after Satyajit Ray's debut feature *Pather Panchali*, which became a surprise hit at the box office that year.

Neel Akasher Neechey (1959)

There are very few films in Mrinal Sen's filmography that were commercial successes. His second film, *Neel Akasher Neechey*, is one of them. Produced by the legendary singer and composer Hemanta Mukherjee, *Neel Akasher Neechey* had some hit songs and beautiful cinematography. The film is about the sweet and innocent relationship between a Chinese hawker and a Bengali housewife. Despite its popularity, *Neel Akasher Neechey* also has the distinction of being banned by the Indian government because at the time, the first round of border clashes had erupted on the India-China border.

Baishey Shravana (1960)

It was with *Baishey Shravana* that Mrinal Sen truly arrived on the scene. The title of the film literally translates to 'the twenty-second day of the month of Shravana'. This date is familiar to most Bengalis as Nobel laureate Rabindranath Tagore's death anniversary as per the Bengali calendar. Since 1941, when Tagore passed away, the date has been one of mourning. In Mrinal-da's film, the date is the wedding anniversary of two villagers whose lives are far removed from the world that Tagore occupied and wrote about. Mrinal-da's hero and heroine look like an odd couple—a middle-aged, plain-looking man and his much younger and beautiful wife. Their relationship unfolds against the backdrop of a devastating famine. If Tagore is familiar as an inherited memory for Bengalis, so was the famine, which had ravaged Bengal a number of times in the past. The camera's gaze shows how hunger and helplessness during the famine corrode the relationship between a man and his wife, destroying their happiness, mutual respect and even trust. In one of my discussions with him, Mrinal-da summed up the film succinctly in three lines, almost like a haiku:

'The man was no villain.
The woman was all grace.
It was a cruel time.'

Baishey Shravana was indeed a cruel film depicting a cruel time, but it also marked the arrival of a great and unconventional film-maker.

At the time of its release, the title led to a bit of a controversy. The fact that there is not even a passing reference to Tagore in *Baishey Shravana* irked the Central Board of Film Certification. Mrinal Sen was told to change the title, which he refused to do. The back and forth between Mrinal-da and the CBFC continued for a few months. Needless to say, Mrinal Sen won the dual.

Akash Kusum (1965)

With the success of *Neel Akasher Neechey*, three films followed in quick succession—*Punascha, Abasheshe* and *Pratinidhi*—

but these did little for the director. Their only credit is that they earned back the production expenses and did not push the director into oblivion. The Mrinal Sen who dreamt of making films that exposed the innate hypocrisies in our urban societies was yet to arrive. It was with *Akash Kusum* that we got our first glimpse of the Mrinal Sen who would be known as the stormy petrel of Bengal's film industry.

Akash Kusum was unlike anything seen in Bengali cinema till the time. It showed the bourgeois society of Calcutta and the vaulting ambition of a middle class that aspired to the good things of life and overreached. At the heart of the film is the story of a relationship between a young woman and man, but one that is built on deceit. The first time I saw *Akash Kusum*, I had just become a college student, having got into Calcutta's most prestigious institution of higher learning, Presidency College. I'm not sure I understood the film back then. When I saw it a few years later, its stylish visual storytelling took my breath away. Mrinal-da's use of freeze frames—which was a novelty to much of the Bengali audience at the time—gave the film a staccato pace. During one of our many chats, he told me that he got the idea of using freeze frames from some experimental French films he'd chanced upon before making *Akash Kusum*. For me, one of the most unforgettable scenes from the film is when the hero, played by Soumitra Chatterjee, climbs up to the terrace, looks at the city sprawled before him and exclaims, 'Bloody hell, one day I will buy up the whole city!' I remember a shiver ran down my spine when I heard that dialogue because it radiated a kind of naked ambition and greed that was unfamiliar to us at the time. Names like Harshad Mehta and Gautam Adani were many decades away, and for me, that scene in *Akash Kusum* remains a harbinger of a future in which the city is characterized by the recklessness and avarice of such men. As the years unfolded and we heard of scams and schemes that earned ambitious young men mindboggling amounts of money, I'd think of *Akash Kusum*.

At the time, *Akash Kusum* divided the Bengali film fraternity into the Satyajit Ray faction and the Mrinal Sen faction. Ray and his camp insisted the film was a take-off from the Aesopian fable of the crow's desire to pass off as a peacock by adding some feathers to its wings, Sen insisted that it was a reflection of our society and was based on a literary work by a contemporary writer. This epistolary battle continued for two months and Sen matched Ray stroke for stroke. For a struggling director with barely any commercial success to his name to be pitted against the country's most brilliant cinematic mind was a formidable achievement.

However, all the controversy did not bring revenue and *Akash Kusum* was a failure. In fact, it fared so badly at the box office that Mrinal Sen had to briefly leave the Bengali film industry and relocate to Odisha to make a small-budget film, *Matira Manisha* (1966). Based on an award-winning novel by Kalindi Charan Panigrahi, the state's most respected literary figure, it was the portrayal of an affluent village family of two brothers. Again, true to his nature, Sen made the younger son a rebel and his storyline did not follow the original novel. This enraged the writer's admirers and particularly the local academics. The market for vernacular films was a small one, and in the commercial circuit too, the film did not do well. But outside Odisha, *Matira Manisha* was critically appreciated, and even won the President's award for best film in Odia.

Bhuvan Shome (1969)

In the 1960s a whole generation of creative minds was being inspired by leftist ideology—Mrinal-da's friends and comrades included the likes of director and screenwriter Ritwik Ghatak, and actor and playwright Utpal Dutt—to create art that was idealistic and rooted in reality. This is what would, in the 1970s, inspire the Indian New Wave, which is, to my mind, our most successful film movement. It started with *Bhuvan Shome.*

There is something interesting I've noted about Mrinal-da's work—at the end of each decade and the beginning of a new one, he almost always reinvented himself. This trend started with *Baishey Shravana* and was followed with *Bhuvan Shome*. The film is about a middle-aged, straitlaced Indian Railways bureaucrat Bhuvan Shome (played by Utpal Dutt) who meets a vivacious young woman, Gauri (Suhasini Mulay), while on a holiday. The titular Bhuvan Shome, or Shome Sahab, gradually loses all the trappings that grant him gravitas and has to ultimately let a ticket collector's fiancée, Gauri, take the lead. In the sand dunes of Gujarat, while on a hunting safari, Shome finds himself in a series of ignominious situation, such as being chased by an enraged buffalo or trying to shoot using the wrong end of the gun. By the end of the film, he's a much mellowed man, who has known helplessness and been humbled by circumstances. There's a poignant scene in which he hands over the hard-earned trophy of a bird to Gauri as a parting gift, thus endearing himself to the audience.

However, *Bhuvan Shome* is not a simple story of a boring bureaucrat being saved by a village belle (as Satyajit Ray summarized it). At the end of his holiday, Shome Sahab returns to his old world, where he is a prisoner of the trappings of his status. He's also plagued by a question—how does his decision to help Gauri's dishonest fiancé measure against his own lifelong crusade against corruption? Has he actually ended up helping corrupt practices by reinstating the unscrupulous young man?

If memory serves me, I saw *Bhuvan Shome* with my whole family during the autumnal festive season, and all of us enjoyed this film, which stands out for being light-hearted, despite being a 'Mrinal Sen film'. Going to the movies felt like a picnic back then, and after seeing the film, we talked delightedly about how every actor—even a serious actor like Shekhar Chatterjee, who plays a bullock cart driver—infused their scenes with rustic wit and humour. Another unexpected breath of fresh air was Mrinal-da's use of animation, a technique that was associated with children's films at the time. I still remember the delightful impression of the opening and closing of the swing door of Shome Sahab's chamber, and the fully stacked 'in' tray getting emptied as the 'out' tray fills up. The animation was superbly executed by Ram Mohan, who was one of Indian cinema's first animators.

Bhuvan Shome went on to become a super-hit, both artistically and commercially. It is today considered the launch pad for the Indian New Wave.

The Calcutta Trilogy: *Interview* (1971), *Calcutta 71* (1972) and *Padatik* (1973)

Interview is the story of a hapless young man who is in search of a decent suit, which he needs because he has to appear for a job interview. Both *Bhuvan Shome* and *Interview* are stories of a new and independent India. They point to the contradictions inherent in our desire to hold on to a colonial legacy while attempting to develop a distinctly modern Indian identity. However, the two films are poles apart since the two stories are very different in terms of backdrop, tone, structure and style. You can see in these two films, which came right after one another, that Mrinal-da had found the subject that would effectively be his obsession for the rest of his career: the urban middle class. While he has made films on rural and urban poverty as well as destitution, it's when Mrinal-da trained his gaze on the middle class that something special invariably came through. From *Akash Kusum* to *Chorus*, every film explores middle-class dreams and how they can be crushed. He posed uneasy questions in his films, but gave no answers. He was relentless in making his audience uncomfortable.

Interview also marks the beginning of another obsession: the city of Calcutta. The success of this film emboldened Mrinal Sen to make *Calcutta 71* and *Padatik*. Both these films were made at the height of what is popularly known as the Naxalite movement. The entire state was in turmoil as the ultra-left student agitators tried to seize power through armed insurrections. The supreme leader of the movement, Charu Majumdar, proclaimed his doctrine *of khatam* or total annihilation of class enemies. The state responded by unleashing terror against terror, and soon enough Calcutta became a battlefield, and the city was in the grip of a near civil war. Sen was in a quandary; he knew he had to react in his own way but was not sure which wing of the left to support. At this juncture, a friendly producer offered him a blank cheque and *Calcutta 71* was born.

Structurally, it is Sen's most complicated film. He chose three short stories, one each from the preceding three decades, showing the onward path of mounting poverty and exploitation. The final part starts with a party scene and ends with another fantasy. All three parts are independent and unrelated to each other; yet a pattern emerges as the film moves towards its climax. *Calcutta 71* begins with a young boy on a misty morning, standing in an empty Calcutta Maidan making a statement like the Greek chorus, then the camera shifts to a brief courtroom farce and a fantasy sequence. At the end of the film, we again see the boy running down a road with piles of dead bodies. His journey ends in Maidan on a misty winter morning, just as it had started in the opening sequence.

The whole experience was, as one critic had commented—unnerving.

Padatik, the last film of the trilogy, is like an expression of Sen's own dilemma framed in celluloid. His hero Sumit, a jail-breaking urban guerrilla, who dares to articulate his doubts about some issues to the central leadership of the Naxalite movement, is immediately dubbed a counter-revolutionary and his own party workers begin to hunt him down. When he is making one last, desperate attempt to escape, we can hear the sound of an approaching police van on the soundtrack.

This tightly made ninety-odd-minute-long film deserved a better fate, but its creator, like its protagonist, had already become a persona non grata for expressing his unhappiness over the happenings and asking uncomfortable questions. I used to tell Mrinal-da, like *Akash Kusum*, *Padatik* too was made much before its time. He silently agreed but argued that making it a few years later would have made it a chapter in history. He wanted the youth who lived amidst the violence of the Naxalite movement to ask themselves what they were out to achieve.

All in all, the Calcutta trilogy does offer some outstanding commentary about middle-class youth. These films also established Mrinal Sen as the voice of a generation as well as one of our greatest film-makers. It is interesting to note that one of the biopics on Mrinal Sen to commemorate his birth centenary is titled *Padatik*.

Chorus (1974)

The Calcutta trilogy could have been a quartet, but *Chorus*, despite Mrinal-da's ambitious plans, ended up being a very different film. *Chorus* begins like a fairy tale and ends up being a hard-hitting social satire. It critiques systems that have been corrupted and speaks of the effect that lack of idealism has on a society, particularly upon the youth. The film earned Mrinal-da a host of awards, including the Golden Lotus at home as well as prizes from the prestigious international film festivals of Berlin and Moscow. For me, though, the cocktail of fairy tale and social satire felt discordant. His co-scriptwriter Mohit Chattopadhyay's penchant for absurd drama and the highly stylized acting of stage veterans such as Utpal Dutt and Shekhar Chatterjee make *Chorus*, for me, one of the weakest of Mrinal-da's films on Calcutta. A big chunk of the audience felt as I did and didn't connect with the film and its gimmicks. My favourite story about *Chorus* is about how during a show in Calcutta, the audience demanded a subtitled print, complaining that the film was going over their heads!

But critics applauded *Chorus* for its stylization. It won many awards—starting with the Best Film by the National Award Jury, Best Cinematography and also Best Music Direction. The less amusing aspect of this film is that *Chorus* was a financial disaster for Mrinal-da, who had produced the film after taking out a bank loan at a high interest rate.

Back to the Roots: *Mrigayaa* (1976), *Oka Oori Katha* (1977)

Shaken by the commercial failure of *Chorus*, Mrinal-da left the city and turned to explore a different constituency—life in our villages. *Mrigayaa*, with Mithun Chakraborty as a tribal youth and Mamata Shankar as his wife, is about the couple's fight for self-respect and a grim story of rural exploitation. The individual battles that we saw in the Calcutta trilogy here become a battle fought by an entire community. It is a simple story intelligently told with some stunning camera tricks and his mandatory gimmicks. *Mrigayaa* is probably better known as Mithun Chakraborty's debut film.

Mrinal-da's next film was *Oka Oori Katha*, based on Munshi Premchand's story *Kafan*, but made in Telugu. The film is a scathing commentary on rural destitution and social injustice. It won the Special Jury Prize (Karlovy Vary IFF) and the Best Feature Film in Telugu at the 25th National Film Awards. The citation said—'for successfully transforming Premchand's story *Kafan* into a scathing commentary on rural destitution and social injustice; for projecting through powerful performances of its leading characters, the degradation and brutalisation of human beings, for its sincere commitment to the cause of the downtrodden; for its fervent impassioned appeal to the conscience of humanity'.

Ek Din Pratidin (1979)

The rural interlude did not inspire Mrinal-da for long. He returned to Calcutta and made *Parashuram* (1979), which was about urban pavement dwellers. By this time, Mrinal-da was a towering figure in the world of parallel cinema. Every film was winning awards and accolades, both within the country and in many prestigious film festivals across the continents. But creatively, he was dissatisfied. It was Gita Boudi who suggested he move out of the familiar frame of left-wing intellectualism and find new authors and new stories. The result was a stunner of a film—*Ek Din Pratidin*.

Based on a novel by Amalendu Chakraborty and with a script written by Mrinal-da, *Ek Din Pratidin* is set in a dilapidated old house in north Calcutta, which is home to a lower-middle-class family of six. One evening, the family's sole breadwinner—a young woman—doesn't return home. What follows is less of a story and more of an exploration. Through the anxiety and helplessness of each family member, the reaction of curious neighbours and the inevitable bickering, Mrinal-da shows the hypocrisy of prevailing social attitudes. We see the intolerable reality that this family must inhabit and from which there is no escape. At the end of the film, as dawn breaks and the girl returns, no one dares ask her the reason for her absence. Not a word is said on where she had spent the night. It is a startlingly modern and progressive take on Mrinal-da's part.

Ek Din Pratidin premiered in the Indian Panorama section of the Filmotsav 1980 in Bangalore, and blew the audience away. I can say this with confidence because I was there. After the screening, while the applause was still ringing and Mrinal-da was coming out of the auditorium, one well-dressed respectable-looking gentleman caught hold of the director. Practically prostrating at Mrinal-da's feet, he said, 'Mrinal-da, I beg you, you must tell me, what happened to the girl that night? Where did she go?' Grinning, Mrinal-da helped him to his feet and said, 'My dear sir, I have made this film for you to watch and suffer, because you will never find the answer to your question.' And with that, he nonchalantly walked out of the hall.

Ek Din Pratidin made decent collections at the box office and brought Mrinal-da many awards—Best Direction award at the National Awards of 1980, Best Editor award and also the Best Regional Film (Bengali). None of us could imagine that a decade later Satyajit Ray would pick up this film to attempt yet another skirmish with Sen. In a letter to Chidananda Dasgupta, his friend and well-known film critic, Ray launched a scathing attack on Sen, saying *Ek Din Pradin* was an example of 'shoddy film-making' and criticized Sen for not knowing what happened to the girl. Mrinal-da had a hearty laugh when he heard Ray's comments and gave a statement defending his style, but this time he did not allow the incident to build up into a full-length skirmish as it had with *Akash Kusum*. But more about the Ray–Sen war of words in the next chapter.

Akaler Sandhane (1980)

This was another one of those films with which Mrinal-da was reinventing himself. *Akaler Sandhane* brought the audience face to face with an India that most of us try to ignore. The film opens with a journey. A busload of effervescent young people are going for an outdoor shoot. They're going to shoot at a village, and the film within the film is about the terrible famine of 1943. As the shoot progresses, the director realizes that 1943 has somehow gate-crashed into the lives of the poverty-ravaged villagers of the present. Unable to face this reality, the director withdraws from the scene.

The brilliance of *Akaler Sandhane* is that it unfolds simultaneously from three perspectives. There's the viewpoint of the group of actors who have come to work but also intend to enjoy an outdoor shoot experience. Then there are the poverty-stricken villagers, waiting to be given a place in the shoot, a free meal, and to earn some money. Finally, there's the director who has the audacity to want to shoot a story based on the ravages of famine, without knowing just how soul-crushing hunger can be. Watching *Akaler Sandhane*, I felt Mrinal-da had truly found the balance between cinema as a weapon to fight social evil and cinema as a medium of entertainment.

Akaler Sandhane won the Grand Jury Prize at Berlin. What followed was a golden period (barring the unimpressive *Chaalchitra*, which was made the following year in 1981).

Kharij (1982)

Kharij earned a jury prize at the Cannes Film Festival, but in my opinion, its greatest achievement was the impact it had on contemporary Bengali society.

Since the late 1960s, it was commonplace to find ten- to twelve-year-olds, usually boys, working as full-time domestic help in a middle-class family. These children worked tirelessly all day, ate meagre meals and did not dare complain. Some families gave the child the opportunity to study, but in most cases, this didn't go beyond the child learning enough to be able to write down names and telephone numbers. *Kharij* changed this status quo.

Little Palan works as a servant—the impolite and politically incorrect term is relevant because he isn't given the dignity implied in the term 'domestic help'—for an affluent middle-class family. He sleeps in the kitchen and works with an invisible presence in the home. One chilly winter night, the boy dies of carbon monoxide poisoning. This comes as an unpleasant shock to his employers, who are a young and civilized couple, brilliantly portrayed by Anjan Dutt and Mamata Shankar. A guilt-stricken Anjan (his character is also named Anjan in the film) tries to exonerate himself with broken sentences—'He was like a member of the family' or 'What is our fault?' Mamata Shankar, also called Mamata in the film, even tries to place the onus on the landlord, saying there was no ventilation system in the kitchen. Anjan can't admit to his own indifference and the part it played in inflicting cruelty upon Palan. A silent spectator in the commotion following Palan's death is another little boy, who like him works in a neighbouring house.

When Palan's father arrives, you hope for some class warfare and to see Palan's employers get their comeuppance. However, Mrinal-da didn't let the audience off so easily. At the simple funeral organized for Palan, the tension thickens but nothing happens. After the funeral, Palan's father leaves with a polite and dignified goodbye. Even one scene of confrontation would have felt cathartic for an audience. Instead, Mrinal Sen's camera imprints the father's behaviour upon the audience's memory, branding the entire bhadralok community of Calcutta.

I remember an interesting sidelight. The premiere show of the film was attended by the then chief minister of West Bengal, Mr Jyoti Basu, the quintessential bhadralok. After watching the film, the CM had commented, 'The film is excellent, but it is too grim to be popular.' He was right. The film did not do well. But it did have an impact. A journalist friend, who was at that time based in Mumbai, was so conscience-stricken after watching the film that he suddenly remembered the boy who worked in his home. 'I hope we give our boy a blanket in November,' he told his wife, forgetting momentarily that blankets are not necessary in Mumbai's balmy, tropical warmth.

Even if *Kharij* wasn't a hit, its impact was for everyone to see—within a few years the trend of keeping young children as domestic help died out.

Khandhar (1983)

Dubbed one of the best films at the Cannes Film Festival that year, *Khandhar* is a heart-breaking story about an insecure generation of young men and women. For me, it is the last truly great work by Mrinal-da.

The story of *Khandhar* comes from a well-known short story, *Telenapota Abishkar*, written in the mid-1930s by Premendra Mitra, an eminent Bengali literary figure. Mrinal-da contemporized it and made a film about a disillusioned generation that has turned away from idealism and embraced escapism. Three young men—Dipu (Pankaj Kapur), Anil (Annu Kapoor) and Subhash (Naseeruddin Shah)—head out of the city and decide to have a weekend retreat at a desolate village where there is no electricity, no running water or any other urban comfort. Dipu has ancestral property in that village, and when the trio get there, they realize the once-palatial mansion is now a ruin. Living in one wing of this crumbling palatial house is an old relative of Dipu, a blind and bedridden widow (played by Gita Boudi). Her only companion is her daughter Jamini (Shabana Azmi).

While exploring the house and the village, the three men pick up a little gossip about the old woman and Jamini. It seems that at one point a young tourist named Niranjan had come to the village, much like them, and then offered to marry Jamini. He used their hospitality, promised to return, but once he left, he never came back. The old lady continues to hope Niranjan will return to marry her daughter. By a cruel twist of fate, when Dipu and Subhash go to pay a courtesy call to the old lady, she is convinced that Subhash is the elusive Niranjan. Calling him close, she begs him to marry Jamini and take her away. To everyone's shock, Subhash accepts the proposal. It's partly to not disappoint the old woman and also because pretending to be Niranjan gives him greater access to photograph the house (Subhash is a photographer by profession).

Jamini seems to understand what is happening but still plays along. She becomes Subhash's guide and model. It's clear that she and Subhash are attracted to one another, but when their holiday draws to a close, the three friends return to their city life while Jamini and her mother remain among the ruins. At the end of the film, we see Subhash working in his studio. The camera pans to show a big blow-up of Jamini hanging on one wall. Whether this is to indicate Jamini remaining fresh and vibrant in Subhash's mind or that the memory of her has been reduced to just a beautiful photograph that may fade with time and neglect, depends upon the viewer's mindset.

Khandhar brought Mrinal-da many awards, much critical appreciation and many open offers to make new films as he wanted. I see *Khandhar* a little differently. For me, the central figure in the film, Subhash, feels like an extension of Mrinal-da himself. Both look at the world through their viewfinders, represent the middle class, are faithful observers, but they maintain a distance from their subject. Let's not forget that for all his sympathies for the left movement, Mrinal-da never aligned himself with any political party and neither did he become a member of any cultural organization such as Indian People's Theatre Association, which was founded on political beliefs that he shared. Many of his friends were active IPTA members, but Mrinal-da remained an outside supporter.

I remember an interesting conversation with the producer of *Khandhar*. He was a producer who made commercial films but had put in money for a film by Mrinal Sen. I met him at a dinner following the National Awards ceremony, proudly moving around, accepting accolades. I asked him, 'Will you be producing Mrinal-da's next film too?' He almost jumped back and said, 'No, no.' Then added a little apologetically, 'I would have, but Mrinal-da does not listen to any suggestion. *Khandhar* could have been a great commercial success, if only Mrinal-da had taken a few of my suggestions. But he is too rigid, he will work only on his own terms.'

This is so true. Mrinal-da made the even French government change their rules when he accepted the offer to make *Genesis*.

Genesis (1986)

Genesis was Mrinal Sen's most ambitious film, a film he thought would keep his legacy alive. In 1982, he received a generous offer from the French government to make a film jointly. The French ministry of culture had a few rules—

any film produced by French government agencies must have French actors, must be made in French and should be at least partially shot in French locations. Sen wanted to shoot the film in India with Indian artists and in an Indian language. The French role would be confined to providing technical support. The issue went up to the level of the French president. Mrinal-da managed to convince him and got all the exemptions he wanted.

For *Genesis*, Mrinal-da got an opportunity that no film-maker from the subcontinent before or after him ever got. A co-production with the French government offered him unrestricted resources, a chance to get the legendary Ravi Shankar as his music composer and the services of a technically competent international crew. Since it was a co-production, Mrinal-da decided the film must have universal appeal. He picked up Friedrich Engels's famous book on the origin of the family, property and the state, combined with it the well-known Bengali author Samaresh Basu's parable-like short story *Uratia*, and with help from an old Marxist friend, Mohit Chattopadhyay, developed a script.

The story centres on a farmer (Naseeruddin Shah) and a weaver (Om Puri) who have to leave their village after a severe drought. Ultimately, they arrive at an abandoned village. The farmer by his hard work makes the place liveable while the weaver enters into a pact with a merchant who provides him equipment, raw materials and food and also buys his products. At this point a woman (Shabana Azmi), the victim of a flood and epidemic, enters their idyllic world. They first resent her presence but allow her to stay. Soon all three become friends and working jointly, they make the desert bloom. But money changes their relationship as both friends start to give the woman presents and desire her. She becomes pregnant but refuses to identify the father. The two friends become sworn enemies and turn their flourishing world into a desert again.

Mrinal-da used the Biblical term 'Genesis' as the title of the film to emphasize the continuous process of construction and destruction within any society and blended it with the Marxist axiom that exploitation of the working class would continue if they failed to unite.

Mrinal-da found a location in Jaisalmer to his liking. It was a deserted village, very close to the border, with beautiful sand dunes and superb sunlight effects. It seemed it was just a matter of time before a masterpiece emerged. But the film was doomed from the start. Locals had warned Mrinal-da that the village he had chosen was haunted and cursed. Mrinal-da had never believed in such grandma's tales nor encouraged superstitious belief, so he did not heed the warnings. But he admitted later that each day's shooting had posed a new problem. Misfortune followed him and his unit during and after the film.

In the climax scene, Mrinal-da wanted to show the total demolition of the settlement. The Government of India offered him the help of the Border Security Force. The whole operation was successfully carried out, but one hour after the 'all clear' signal, when Mrinal-da with his Italian director of photography and his French sound recordist went to visit the spot, suddenly, a bomb literally burst in their faces, injuring all of them. They had to be admitted to a local hospital for treatment. When I asked him about this incident, he replied, 'I am still not sure whether it was an accident, sabotage or an act of God.' A strange admission from a confirmed Marxist.

The movie ended up becoming heavily political, something I feel became an additional curse. Critics lauded or condemned it, according their ideological stands, which was rather unfortunate. Naseeruddin Shah attacked the film violently, calling it a 'load of crap'. Ravi Shankar was also unhappy. He once said humorously, 'Only Mrinal can engage me and keep me sitting pretty.' In the end, in spite of its technical excellence, the film failed to make an impression.

His Indian partner, Ramaswamy, ran into major financial difficulties and almost went bankrupt. In distress, he could not pay enough attention to the film and failed to find a distributor, so the film was never commercially released in India. Because of the French collaboration, Mrinal-da could not submit it for National Awards or Indian Panorama. So barring a few private screenings here and there and a late-night screening on Doordarshan, the film remained out of bounds for his countrymen. This hit Mrinal-da the hardest—his inability to show his work to his own people.

In my discussions with him, I found Mrinal-da strangely unenthusiastic about this attempted masterpiece. Perhaps he too recognized the hand of providence, that something had gone wrong somewhere.

Ek Din Achanak (1989)

Mrinal-da ended the eighties with *Ek Din Achanak*, which makes for an interesting companion piece to *Ek Din Pratidin*. A retired professor of history leaves his home, ostensibly for a walk, but does not come back. There was no quarrel, no exchange of angry words with his family members before this quiet exit, and yet the professor chooses to leave everything behind. No one can understand why. Eventually, we find that all his books have been removed from his study. In the empty room, the professor's wife, son and two daughters talk about him, all of them trying to understand what went wrong. Their conversation slowly turns into a session of confessions. Ultimately, the eldest daughter says, 'When a man comes to realize that he is an ordinary human being and that is the way he will have to live the rest of his days, his life becomes nothing but an endless agony. He can neither start afresh nor change the past.' As the mother observes, Man's ultimate tragedy is that he can live only once.

What makes *Ek Din Achanak* particularly poignant is that this sentiment was one that Mrinal-da shared. In that sense, the film is deeply autobiographical at an emotional level. Of course, Mrinal-da didn't leave his world in the same way. In his last years, when he was bedridden and beginning to lose his memory, I often wondered whether he remembered the professor from *Ek Din Achanak* who feared becoming irrelevant. I think one of the reasons why I made it a point to visit him was that I didn't want to feel he was being neglected by the world around him. For some of us, Mrinal-da will always be relevant, and no matter how much his beloved Calcutta changes, it will perhaps (unlike the professor's study) always contain traces of him because of the films he set in the city.

Mahaprithibi (1991)

The fall of the Soviet empire was like an earthquake for Mrinal-da and his socialist friends, and the aftershock was evident in *Mahaprithibi*. For many in his generation, the political philosophy of scientific socialism had been the ultimate truth, and Mrinal-da admitted to being acutely depressed when the Soviet Union was dissolved over the course of three years, between 1988 and 1991.

The story of *Mahaprithibi* came from his young friend and protégé Anjan Dutt, and just like its name, it has a little bit of everything. Spanning over two decades, it maps the trials and tribulations of a family where one son is a Naxalite, another is looked upon as an escapist who runs away to Germany, and a daughter who is mentally ill. Chronicling these lives is a mother who ultimately chooses suicide over this life. *Mahaprithibi* was made in 1991 and was critically appreciated. However, like many of Mrinal-da's films, it did not impress the average cinegoer. I'm one of them. I just could not link the reunion of Germany with the suicide of an old lady in Calcutta. Maybe I am not sensitive enough.

Writing about this film a few years later, Mrinal-da had said, 'Policies, ideas, values and morals changed overnight. Deep within, I now realize I am a bundle of confusion.' I agree with his self-analysis.

Antareen (1993)

Only one person could have brought together Saadat Hasan Manto and Rabindranath Tagore, and that was Mrinal-da. Blending two stories by these literary icons, he brought to life a lyrical film—*Antareen*. The ethereal bearing of Dimple Kapadia and her telephonic conversations with Anjan Dutt add a surreal beauty to the film, not expected from a Mrinal Sen movie. I call it 'the *Kshudhito Pashan* of Calcutta'. *Antareen* is like a poem on celluloid. It won the Best Bengali Film Award in the National Awards of 1993.

Aamaar Bhuvan (2002)

Mrinal-da's last film ended up being a hymn to simplicity. The film-maker set aside the complex cinematic language that he was famous for and opted for a story in which poverty is seen without scars or ugliness. Most critics found it almost too simplistic, touching on naivety. I used to believe it was a very ordinary film by Mrinal-da's standards, but looking back on *Aamaar Bhuvan* now, I wonder if it was Sen's way of paying tribute to his lifelong friend and critic Ritwik Ghatak. In Ghatak's last film *Jukti, Takko Aar Gappo*, Ghatak, playing the role of a burnt-out, alcoholic intellectual, would mutter, 'Everything is burning, the universe is burning, I am burning.' The dialogue seems to echo T.S. Eliot's famous poem 'The Waste Land' and appears to be referenced in the opening sequence of *Aamaar Bhuvan*.

Mrinal-da also acknowledged his admiration of Charlie Chaplin by incorporating certain sequences from Chaplin's movies. I wonder now if *Aamaar Bhuvan* was very consciously a swansong, one in which he tried to settle his imagined accounts and debts.

The film went on to win an award in the Cairo Film Festival, and although this did bring Mrinal-da much joy, it wasn't enough for him to pick up the director's megaphone again in his remaining years.

*

I'm reminded now of a Sunday morning at Mrinal-da's Beltala Road flat, two years after he'd made *Antareen*. In those two years, he had toyed with many ideas, including *Bhubaneswari*, based on a novel by Bimal Kar, which he had actually developed into a proper script, but he did not seriously pursue any of these ideas. There was no shortage of producers or offers from well-known writers with their works, but Mrinal-da was strangely reluctant. That morning when I arrived, he was sitting alone, with his pipe, an empty teacup before him. Gita Boudi greeted me with her usual warmth and immediately sent for two more cups of black tea, our best stimulant for starting a conversation.

'Mrinal has been unusually lazy of late,' she confided to me. 'He is not working on anything seriously.'

I had also found him to be somewhat quiet in our recent conversations, which of late seemed to be about all things other than films. That day, I tried to get him back to talking about cinema.

'You have made twenty-five films in forty years,' I told him. 'You have never aimed to be a commercial film-maker, so I think it is an excellent strike rate. But are you satisfied with your achievement, or do you feel that some melodies remain unheard?'

Mrinal-da lit his pipe and replied pensively, 'No artist is ever fully satisfied with his creation. There are some films that I wanted to make but could not. I shall probably never be able to make them, but do I regret not making them? I am not sure.'

'How about telling me something about those projects?' I asked.

He took some time to reply. 'One film that I could not make in spite of considerable research and a well-designed treatment was on the Kayyur uprising. Have you heard the name Kayyur before?'

When I admitted to being ignorant, he told me how five boys had plotted an armed agrarian revolt in this small village in Kerala. 'Ultimately, they could not achieve anything. All of them were caught red-handed. Four of them were hanged as they were above twenty-five. The fifth one was spared as he was only fifteen. But their courage and sacrifice became legendary. In the 1940s, every Indian would speak about the Kayyur heroes. IPTA composed songs about them.' Mrinal-da added that the legendary political leader of Kerala, E.M.S. Namboodiripad, had requested him to make a film on this saga.

'But what was the snag?' I wanted to know.

Mrinal-da smiled and started telling me what happened when he went to Kayyur for research and to select locations. 'A huge crowd gathered around me. They even brought a very old woman who could hardly speak to meet me. She was the mother of one of the martyrs. She had a wonderfully wrinkled face, and I immediately decided to start the film by training the camera on her face. But then something strange happened. I noticed an elderly man trying to approach me, but the crowd was not allowing him to come anywhere near me. Later I was told that he was the youngest rebel who had been spared the gallows because he was a minor. Now he was an outsider in his village because he toed the CPI line in a CPI (M)-dominated area! Political tangles got in the way of making this film,' Mrinal-da said with a sigh.

We sat silently for a while. Suddenly Mrinal-da said, 'Since you are interested, I can tell you about one of my stray thoughts. These images keep coming back to my mind. The storyline is like this—near the international border, there is a shack where an old woman runs a teashop. Motor mechanics and truck drivers who carry consignments from one country to another are her clientele. One winter night, as she is about to close her shop, a young woman comes running to her for shelter. She is far too thin, seems to be suffering from malnutrition and is in an advanced stage of pregnancy. The old woman asks her about her family, about the father of the child but gets no response. Before daybreak, in this no-man's land amidst the hooting of trucks and the drunken brawls of drivers and mechanics, a child is born, a child without a father, perhaps without a nation. And yet this birth becomes a significant event. Some of these ideas have haunted me for a long time, I even wrote a possible treatment, but could not develop it into a fully-fledged script. I could not work out the rest of the story, so the film was never made.'

I asked, 'Is it *Genesis 2.0*?'

'Maybe, maybe not. But honestly, I do not know.'

The empty chairs had started to fill up. It was time for his Sunday morning durbar. I had no interest in joining the crowd and got up.

'Just a moment,' Mrinal-da said. 'Let me give you some more food for thought. You know, sometimes I see myself going back to that village where I shot *Akaler Sandhane*. I go there alone, twenty years after I was there with my full team. This time, my journey is all by myself, no production unit or camera. I just want to see the village, see how it has changed in these twenty years. As I walk through the village, I meet an old man and ask, "A tall, thin, dark man came to shoot a film here many years ago. His name was probably Mrinal Sen. Do you still remember him?" I haven't been able to figure out his response. Wouldn't it be an interesting last film? My last testament? The film will complete the circle that started with *Baishey Shravana*. How do you like the idea?'

Mrinal Sen did not make this film either. He never went back to see that location. In the twenty-first century, Mrinal-da, already ageing, seemed to be losing his zest. He became increasingly alone; Satyajit Ray and Ritwik Ghatak passed into history, making Mrinal Sen the elder statesman of Indian cinema. He kept himself busy with activities such as inaugurating everything from book fairs to film festivals, and occasional parliamentary duties. Film-making slowly receded into the background. We, the people closest to him, began to realize there would be no more path-breaking movies.

But in 2002, when he was approaching his eightieth birthday, to our great surprise, without any elaborate discussion or preparation, something typical of his film-making, Mrinal-da announced he would be making another film. He chose a location in a nearby village and made *Aamar Bhuvan*. It was a serene hamlet with a few hutments and a few nicely constructed houses and lots of greenery. Upon this idyllic setting, Mrinal Sen, the great and unconventional film-maker, stamped his world view. In the very first shot, the screen is filled with these words in big, capital letters: 'THE WORLD IS BREAKING UP, BURNING, DISINTEGRATING; STILL MEN LIVE HERE IN LOVE, COMPASSION AND EMPATHY.'

3

The Ultimate Duel

It all began with a series of letters that were printed in *The Statesman*, Calcutta's most prestigious English daily at the time.

In 1965, Mrinal Sen made *Akash Kusum*. It is the story of a young man of a lower middle-class background who falls in love with a woman from an affluent family. Fearing rejection, he presents himself to her as an upcoming but successful businessman. She believes him, which means he has to continue the charade. He begins to borrow heavily from a rich friend and tries some shady, quick-fix methods to become rich overnight. In the end, he fails miserably and loses whatever he has, including the girl.

Based on a story written by Ashish Barman—a distant relative of Satyajit Ray—*Akash Kusum* became a powerful exposé of urban consumerism, thanks to Mrinal Sen's film-making. Sen used a light-hearted style to lead the unsuspecting audience to a grim climax. As a social commentary, it hit hard, which is probably why *Akash Kusum* failed, both in terms of commercial and critical responses.

Contemporaries such as Santi P. Choudhury, a well-known documentary film-maker, hailed *Akash Kusum* as the first truly urban Bengali movie. Professor

Amalendu Bose, head of the department of English in the University of Calcutta, lamented that the average moviegoer was so engrossed by the hero's antics that he failed to appreciate the tragedy of the story. However, there were many others who disagreed with such opinions.

In his review of *Akash Kusum*, which appeared in *The Statesman* on 23 July 1965, the paper's film critic had observed that 'had the film ended on the same serio-comic mode, probably the audience would have been more sympathetic to the hero', going on to say:

> The revelation of the deception that the hero had been practicing was fit occasion for some high comedy, at the end of which the hero might still have retained, like Don Quixote, his schizophrenic view of the world but we could have got our laughs while in some street-corner of our heart we would have retained as we do for the knight of the woeful countenance—a trace of sympathy, even admiration for this hopeless dreamer.

Barman reacted sharply to this critique. He wrote back:

> We feel a Don Quixote ending for a contemporary story with all its immediacy of the scene would have been totally unconvincing and hence dangerous. For a period piece, no doubt, this could have been a plausible postulate. This cinema mirrors the reality too objectively, with a ruthless precision and lucidity of the images;

> hence it is almost impossible to lend stylised ambiguity of a topical theme. I stress the word 'topical'.

The editor of *The Statesman* thought the matter was over after this sharp exchange of words between his film critic and Ashish Barman, but then came a response from someone who could not be silenced. Satyajit Ray sent his comments and in his inimitable style, he delivered a scathing dismissal of *Akash Kusum*. Ray wrote:

> May I point out that the topicality of the theme in question stretches back into antiquity, when it found expression in that touching fable about the poor deluded crow with a fatal weakness for status symbols. Had Mr Barman known of the fate of this crow he would surely have imparted the knowledge of his protagonist, who now acts in complete ignorance of traditional precepts, with—need I add—fabulous consequences. ... It is almost impossible to lend stylized ambiguity to a topical theme. I stress the word 'topical'.

An enraged Barman responded immediately:

> I am flattered to see that Mr Satyajit Ray, one of the greatest film-makers of the world, has taken note of my letter pertaining to your film critic's review of our film *Akash Kusum*. In his nimble comments however,

> he has mixed up two different aspects of a topical theme; for the topicality of the story does not negate the basic human urges like love, jealousy, hunger, hope or the desire for a better life. What it does is to stamp these basic urges with the contemporary forms and the urgency of a central focus. As far as the question of imparting the precepts of antiquity is concerned, may I remind Mr Ray that great men like Christ, Buddha, and Gandhiji have done the same from the past—evidently with not much success.

At this point, Mrinal Sen entered the fray. While talking about the duel of words years later, Mrinal-da insisted that he began writing not to continue but to close this exchange. He wrote to *The Statesman*:

> I am rather tempted to bring in a champion in this seemingly exciting polemics—Chaplin—who, made much in the image of the poor deluded crow of Aesop's fables, expressed, to quote his own words, 'my conception of the average men, any man, of myself'. His derby, according to him, strove for dignity, his moustache for vanity and so on. And in later years after World War II, when the world was atrociously different—old fatal weakness for status symbols drove Chaplin to kill a dozen women. And I am sure Mr Ray will certainly not doubt the topicality of Chaplin's theme brought out with such mastery

> during the long years of his film career. Was it not this madness, which is so palpable in all Chaplin's works, evident in Don Quixote which yet remained contemporaneous, and in our days do we not share the same aberrations in lesser or greater degree with indeed 'fabulous consequences'? I do not, by any chance, wish to take refuge under the fabled crow's wings and claim to be an Aesop or a Cervantes or Chaplin. I have made a film called *Akash Kusum* and that is all.

Sen's comments did nothing to douse the debate. Missives from Ray, Sen and Barman continued to appear, each one fanning the flames of controversy. Sen sent rejoinders, Ray reacted with unpleasant comments. Sen and Barman insisted *Akash Kusum* was a portrait of contemporary society that reflected the restlessness of the youth, while Ray saw the film as a plain, simple and badly made comedy. The 'Letters to the Editor' column in *The Statesman* started filling up with comments from all quarters. Film buffs and cine-club members such as Barun Chanda commented, 'Mr Satyajit Ray has overlooked the possibility that there are people who can overgrow children's fables, or, better still, translate them into an adult language.' Rajat Roy Choudhury added, 'Mr Satyajit Ray instead of constructively criticising the film *Akash Kusum*, in a roundabout manner pulls its director and story-writer's legs and quibbles with words. Mr Ray himself borrows from old and outdated stories and ideas in his films. How then he can blame anyone for such borrowing?'

As the controversy snowballed, regular readers joined in. One film enthusiast wrote, 'Mr Satyajit Ray's Big Brother attitude towards Mr Mrinal Sen and Ashish Barman is surprising. *Akash Kusum* has contemporaneity in its very theme and not on the surface. Castle building in the air is topical enough.' Another film enthusiast wrote, 'The exchange of letters between Satyajit Ray and Mrinal Sen and Ashish Barman is amusing. In his latest letter (August 21-22) Mr Ray considers himself to be an authority on what he calls "contemporaneity". I doubt it very much after seeing *Kapurush*.'

The very next day a letter was published supporting Ray. Dilip Ghosh wrote, 'Mr Satyajit Ray has rightly classified *Akash Kusum* as a crow-film. Any enlightened viewer will find a very great difference between Chaplin's tramp and Mr Barman's hero whose entire thinking rolls around bluffing.'

This exchange of letters rekindled the audience's interest in seeing the film. One viewer wrote after watching it, 'I have read with interest the letters on *Akash Kusum* and now I have seen the picture and feel constrained to say that it has not been able to retain the reputation of Mr Sen as a film director. It is a commonplace production. Except for some lively dialogue, there is hardly anything praiseworthy.'

On 1 September, *The Statesman* carried a comment on the film by Ray in which the film-maker deliberately used the word 'contemporary' in every sentence and ended the letter with a statement that remains famous for its savagery: 'A crow-film is a crow-film is a crow-film.'

Sen wrote back quickly:

> In trying to derive a 'contemporary moral', Mr Ray by adding three doubtful prefixes, has conveniently reconstructed a famous line which originally belonged to the French film director Jean-Luc Godard: 'A film is a film is a film.' In this connection it may be interesting to note that Mr Godard, unlike Mr Ray, prefers to remain amoral and will perhaps 'suffer' many human frailties, including 'persistent lying' even 'in beds'.

An anguished reader was so provoked by these exchanges that he wrote, 'Only one person does not know how great Mr Satyajit Ray is. That is Mr Ray himself. How else could he stoop to attack a poor colleague so mercilessly?' Another wrote back, 'As a result of this controversy, all that has happened is, a mediocre film has received tremendous publicity and the general public has lost some of its regards [sic] for Mr Ray.'

On 13 September, the management of the newspaper officially brought the matter to a close by declaring no more correspondence on the subject would be published 'as it is nobody's loss, nobody's gain'.

By coincidence, the two film-makers met at a Film Society meeting on the same evening. Ray said to Sen with a smile, 'What a pity it ended too soon. I could have written many more letters.' Sen replied, 'I have neither your firepower, nor your support base. Yet I would have replied to each of them.'

The era of friendship between two greats of Bengali cinema was over. For the next few decades, the two would maintain a frosty distance.

It is still difficult to fathom why Ray launched such a vitriolic attack on Sen. At the start of their careers as film-makers their relationship was quite cordial. Senior to Sen by two years and twelve days, Ray always called him 'Mrinal', while Sen courteously addressed him as 'Manik babu'. In the early 1950s, Sen wrote a book on Chaplin and approached Ray to illustrate the cover of the book. Ray agreed and did not charge anything for this work. In 1961, when Ray was contemplating his first Technicolor film *Kanchenjunga*, Sen suggested the actor N. Viswanathan for the role of the prospective son-in-law. Ray cast him in the role. Similarly, when Sen wanted stage actress Kanika Majumdar as his leading lady in *Punascha* (1961), he sought Ray's help as Ray knew Kanika (both belonging to the Brahmo Samaj community). Ray not only helped convince her, but also put in a word before the contract was finalized. A couple of years later, Ray's wife, Bijoya Ray, helped Sen find a suitable child artist for *Pratinidhi*.

The respect that the two film-makers had for one another was obvious when Ray told his Film Society members that they must see Sen's *Baishey Shravana*. In January 1965, India hosted the International Film Festival in Delhi for which Ray was invited to be the chairman of the international jury. Sen also attended the festival but as an ordinary delegate. In spite of his busy schedule, Ray found time to arrange an out-of-festival screening of *Baishey Shravana* and took it upon himself to invite people for the screening. This was why many international film personalities such as Lindsay Anderson (UK), Georges Sadoul (France), Madame Kawakita (Japan) and a fleet of foreign film critics attended the screening. *Baishey Shravana* got excellent reviews in the international media, and this was the first time Sen got the attention of foreign critics. No one could have foreseen then that within a span of nine months the relationship between Ray and Sen would be irreparably soured.

Almost thirty-five years later, one afternoon Mrinal-da and I were alone in his house and we found an old copy of *The Statesman*. I asked Mrinal-da about the rift between him and Ray. He smiled and said, 'One evening, Manik babu rang me and said, "I won't hurt you, I just want to make some observations on Ashish's story." Naturally, I had no objections. Then in his inimitable style, he wrote something about the story, which was a bit critical. Ashish immediately hit back, which he could have avoided. I need not have reacted but I also joined the fray, initially just for fun. Again Satyajit Ray wrote a letter. Again Ashish replied and I sent in my rejoinder. The whole issue snowballed, more than a hundred people joined the debate and it became a raging battle between antiquity and contemporaneity.'

To my mind, Ray recognized that in Sen he had a rival, and as appreciative as he was of Sen's film-making talent, as a cinephile, it also unsettled him. While Ray belonged to one of Calcutta's most elite families and had enjoyed the benefits of this, Sen was from the backwaters of Faridpur with no social capital to speak of. Ray was an alumnus of Presidency College and Santiniketan; Sen had been a student of science from an ordinary college. Before entering the world of cinema, Ray was already known to be a talented illustrator and had a senior position in an advertising firm. Sen worked as a medical representative. Ray and his friends had formed the Calcutta Film Society. Sen, in contrast, could not afford the membership fee. Ray was a success story with his very first film. Sen had a string of failures till *Bhuvan Shome*.

Despite the lukewarm response it got, I think something about *Akash Kusum* made Ray realize that Sen had succeeded in telling the kind of fable Ray had tried to in *Paras Pathar*, but without much success. *Paras Pathar* came out in 1958 and was about a lowly clerk who chances upon a magical stone and becomes rich. Ray attempted to use it to create a contemporary portrait of Calcutta, but both critics and audiences treated *Paras Pathar* as a simple, light-hearted comedy, a children's film. In contrast, Sen had taken the simple story of *Akash Kusum* and used it to explore the same desire to become rich and was able to link it with issues plaguing the everyday lives of middle-class Calcutta.

Perhaps this is why Ray had insisted *Akash Kusum* should be seen as nothing more than a mere comedy—much like

Paras Pathar had been—and criticized Sen for changing the tone at the end by introducing seriousness to the tale. There's an article by Ray about India's New Wave that has further convinced me that I'm right.

In 1971, Ray wrote in an article on the Indian New Cinema Movement where he came down heavily on Sen. He wrote:

> Among these films, *Bhuvan Shome* is cited widely as an offbeat film which has succeeded with a minority audience. My own opinion is that whatever success it had, has not been because of, but in spite of, its new aspects. It worked because it used some of the most popular conventions of cinema which helped soften the edges of its occasional spiky syntax. These conventions are: a delectable heroine, an ear-filling background score, and a simple, wholesale wish-fulfilling screen story (summary in seven words: Big Bad Bureaucrat Reformed By Rustic Belle).

It's an unfairly harsh and ungenerous take on *Bhuvan Shome*, which only makes sense to me if one sees the review as an analysis by someone who is viewing the work of a rival. Objectively speaking, *Bhuvan Shome* deserves much more than Ray was willing to grant it. Sen was hurt by this criticism from Ray, but he avoided any rejoinder. Perhaps the *Akash Kusum* epistolary war was still fresh in his memory.

However, he did get a chance to settle scores. In 1976, the first compilation of Ray's articles on cinema was published under the title *Our Films, Their Films*. The piece on the Indian New Wave also found a place in the compilation. Sen was asked to review the book and after some hesitation, he agreed. In his review, Sen responded to Ray's critique and wrote: 'All I had tried to do in *Bhuvan Shome* was to try something out-of-the-box, something unconventional, to clear the cobwebs that choked the free flow of ideas in Indian cinema. The film became a huge success—critics lauded it, audience loved it. Naturally, I was happy. People accepted the film for its freshness of approach. Nothing more, nothing less.'

The review appeared with the heading 'His Book, My Comments'. According to Mrinal-da, he got a call from Ray a few days after the review was published. Here's how Mrinal-da remembered the conversation when he recounted it to me.

Ray said, 'You put me to shame, Mrinal.'

Mrinal-da asked Ray if he'd read the review and if he'd liked it.

'Of course, I liked it,' Ray replied. 'I liked it very much.'

'Did you feel I was trying to take a dig at you?' Mrinal-da asked him.

'In just a few parts, but you were surprisingly very mild and respectful.'

'To be honest, I could have taken a harder dig.'

'But you didn't.'

'I was scared of your yes-men.'

Ray had laughed at that.

Mrinal-da said to me, 'I didn't speak for some time and allowed Manik babu to talk. It was a quiet session with him and a long one. At a certain point of time, I asked him, "Don't you feel lonely at times?"'

'Terribly,' Ray replied. 'Why don't you come by one day?'

Mrinal-da promised he would. And that was how, after years of a communication breakdown, two stalwarts of Indian cinema tried to bury the hatchet.

In the years that followed, they often met publicly and shared the stage in various film-related functions. The cordiality was there for everyone to see. For instance, in the late 1970s, both were invited to the Cannes Film Festival one year. Ray arrived in France first and learnt that the event at the main hall demanded invitees wear a dress suit with black bow tie. He had neither. The only alternative was to wear an Indian attire. Messages were exchanged between the Sen and Ray families in Calcutta, and Mrinal-da arrived in Cannes with a set of clothes for Ray.

Still, despite these instances, the distance between Bishop Lefroy Road, Ray's famous residence (the street has since been renamed Satyajit Ray Dharani), and Beltala Road (officially known as Naresh Mitra Sarani), where Mrinal-da spent almost a quarter of a century, could not be reduced. I remember an incident in 1980.

Pather Panchali was celebrating a silver jubilee in 1980. That year, at the International Film Festival of India, a grand celebration was arranged. Ray and his wife were given the status of special guests. It also marked twenty-five years as a film-maker for Mrinal-da, but this was celebrated the following year when the Information and Broadcasting Secretary, Mr A.K. Dutt, came up with the idea of organizing an event to felicitate Mrinal-da. He suggested Ray as the chief guest, and I was tasked with convincing Ray to attend.

My personal equation with Ray was very warm, but I was hesitant to take up this task. I had a feeling it would be difficult to convince Ray to be there for an event felicitating Mrinal Sen. Still, two days after Christmas, I rang up Ray at his home. The conversation went exactly along the lines I had expected. In that beautiful baritone of his, Ray asked me about the preparations for the festival, the entries in the Indian Panorama section and the international films we were expecting to get. I promised that the curation had been excellent. Then, after this small talk, I dropped the big question. 'Will you be free on the evening of the 4th?'

'I think so,' Ray replied. 'Why? Are you planning anything?'

'We're organizing an event to honour Mrinal-da on completing twenty-five years as a film-maker. Would you grace the occasion? Mr Dutt, the Secretary, specially asked if you would—'

'No, Dipankar, leave me out,' he said. 'It won't be possible. There are problems.'

I knew to ask more would be to cross a Lakshman rekha, but I did it anyway. 'What problems, Manik-da? Please do come.'

I can still hear his booming baritone in my ear as he said, 'You won't understand, Dipankar. But it can't be, can't be, can't be.' (*Ta hoi na, ta hoi na, ta hoi na.*)

By this time, the incidents surrounding *Akash Kusum* were more than a decade in the past. Hence, Ray's prickly attitude just didn't make sense. There was something wistful but intense about the way he'd said 'it can't be', and it has stayed with me all these years. Back then, I decided not to tell Mrinal-da about this exchange. It was a professional exchange between Ray and myself, and there was no justification to make it public.

A few years later, while delivering the Guardian Lecture in London, Ray once again made his hostility towards Sen evident when he said, 'Mrinal Sen always hits a safe target', while talking about political content in Indian cinema. When the media asked Mrinal-da for his response, he played it down by joking, 'Ray has hit the safest target: Me.'

Mrinal Sen also made his digs at Ray, but they were milder in comparison. For example, in an article he wrote for the *Illustrated Weekly of India*, Sen wrote, 'While down South, the New Wave Movement was flourishing, in Bengal, it was the era of mythologicals like *Jai Baba Taraknath* and *Joy Baba Felunath*.' *Joy Baba Felunath* was Ray's mystery thriller, made for a younger audience and without any aspirations of artistry.

The bitterness between Ray and Sen lurked under the surface and burst through at unexpected moments. One example is the letter Ray wrote to his old friend and eminent critic Chidananda Dasgupta, just a year before passing away. At the time, he had survived two heart attacks and was becoming more or less bedridden. Writing in June 1991, Ray included a pointed criticism of Sen while commenting on contemporary Indian cinema. 'Mrinal is the prime example of shoddy film-making, specifically for his comment about *Ek Din Pratidin* that he did not know what his leading lady was doing at the dead of night,' he wrote, insisting a film-maker should never be so ignorant about his own characters. Evidently, Ray had lost sight of how progressive and radical it was for Sen to have insisted a woman is not required to give such explanations.

Ray's personal opinion, expressed privately to his friend, became public when Dasgupta released the letter to a national daily. Ray did not object, and many film-lovers wondered whether *Akash Kusum 2.0* would follow. This time, Sen reacted first but with restraint and maturity. On 7 October 1991, he issued a statement in which he said, 'I cannot and shall not be a party to a smear-campaign which normally arises from such a devastating statement reported to be Ray's. After all, none of us are any more in 1965, when over a film of mine, *Akash Kusum*, my writer-friend Ashish Barman unwittingly dragged Ray into a polemic which inevitably prompted me to join the fray and when, immediately after, a minimum of fifty correspondents indulged in a two-month-long battle of words—all in the columns of Calcutta's highly respected English daily *The Statesman*. Such open duel of words was unheard of in the history of Indian cinema. On instant reaction I now wish I could take up points one after another, allegedly to have been put forward by Ray … and raise a civilized debate. But I won't, for fear of disturbing his mental peace on health grounds; he needs to remain calm as much as he needs his daily drugs.'

Sen made it clear that he was holding back out of deference to Ray's declining health, but he did refute some points Ray had made. He concluded his statement with these words: 'Everybody, including Satyajit Ray, is entitled to his likes and dislikes, but none, not even Ray, can set rules for others too.' With this firm stand, he defused the crisis and the controversy petered out. Six months later, an ailing and exhausted Ray passed away.

I don't know whether Ray made a courtesy call to the Sen household when Gita Boudi underwent open-heart surgery, but I do know the Sens visited Ray at Bishop Lefroy Road when, in 1990, news of Ray's ill health reached them. He called me to tell me about that historic meeting. When he went to Ray's house, he found that Nemai Ghosh (Ray's favourite photographer) was also there. At one point, Ray told Ghosh, 'Now you move on, Mrinal and I have to talk.'

'So, what did you talk about?' I asked.

'Well,' Mrinal-da said, 'we talked about so many things.'

I could tell he was being evasive, and I remember telling him that if he didn't want the next generations to gossip about him and Ray, he'd better be honest about this meeting in his memoirs.

In 1992, Satyajit Ray breathed his last. Another decade went by. In 2004, Mrinal Sen finally decided to write his memoir. Before sending the manuscript to his publisher, he called me over and gave me a section to read. It was about that evening. This is all Mrinal-da would share with the world: 'I had a quiet session with him (Ray), a long session—he and I, no one else. He spoke of his intense loneliness and I spoke about my growing physical weakness.'

Ray took the initiative of making sure a photographer recorded the occasion for posterity. The famous photograph is available all over the internet now.

During his last months, Ray spent most of his time in a nursing home. He was in the hospital bed when he received both the Oscar and Bharat Ratna awards. Mrinal-da and Gita Boudi visited him regularly. After each visit, Mrinal-da would tell me, 'See, he will come out of it. I know him too well; this man possesses an indomitable life force.'

There is, however, only so long that one can hold out against that final farewell. I was dismayed to see how intensely Ray's death affected Mrinal-da. 'There is no one left to fight or even to argue with,' he told me, and the anguish in his voice was palpable.

In the summer of 1992, the Cannes Film Festival published the entire set of *Akash Kusum* letters. It was given to delegates and the epistolary duel between Ray and Sen was given a formal place in the history of cinema and in the archives of cinephiles.

It isn't an exaggeration to say Ray and Sen had a peculiar relationship that was marked by an undercurrent of admiration as well as intense rivalry. Both were passionate about cinema, but were diametrically different in the way they understood the art form. Just as their film-making styles were sharply contrasting, so were their tastes. Ray was fond of Hollywood films; Sen's preference was for European cinema. Both were avid readers and had an impressive collection of books, but Ray's preference was for the classics, while Sen was interested in modern literature.

In their films, they explored modern themes, but their treatment was totally different. The contrast between *Pratidwandi* and *Interview* is a good example.

Even when they opted to make films based on the writings of the same author, their selection spoke of their differences. Ray adapted Premchand's *Shatranj Ke Khiladi* and recreated a grand, decadent world of a fading royalty. Sen picked up Premchand's *Kafan* and made it into *Oka Oori Katha*. The Great Bengal Famine of 1943 cast its shadow over both their imaginations, yet there is no similarity between *Ashani Sanket* and *Baishey Shravana* or *Akaler Sandhaney*. In their early years, Ray was lyrical, and he created characters that were subdued and low-pitched; Sen was loud, angry and vocal. Twenty years later, there would be a reversal. In *Jana Aranya*, one can feel Ray's anger and disgust at society while Sen's restraint in *Kharij* is masterful. Sen's admirers had questioned his decision to not include an outburst in the film, especially when the dead boy's father does a polite namaskar at the end. What happened to Sen's famous temper, they asked.

Fundamentally different and yet intrinsically connected, Ray and Sen could not be friends, but they remained one another's companion on their long and illustrious journeys. They enjoyed their duel of words and grappled with the challenges that one posed to the other. It was almost as though there was a glass wall that stood between the two—one that wouldn't be shattered, but through which, despite everything, one kept an eye on the other till the end.

কল্লোল ফিল্মস্-এর নিবেদন
বাইশে শ্রাবণ
পরিচালনা • মৃণাল সেন
সঙ্গীত • হেমন্ত মুখোপাধ্যায়
পরিবেশনা • ছায়ালোক

পূর্বাচল ফিল্মসের
আকাশ কুসুম
আর·ডি·বনশল নিবেদিত
পরিচালনা· মৃণাল সেন

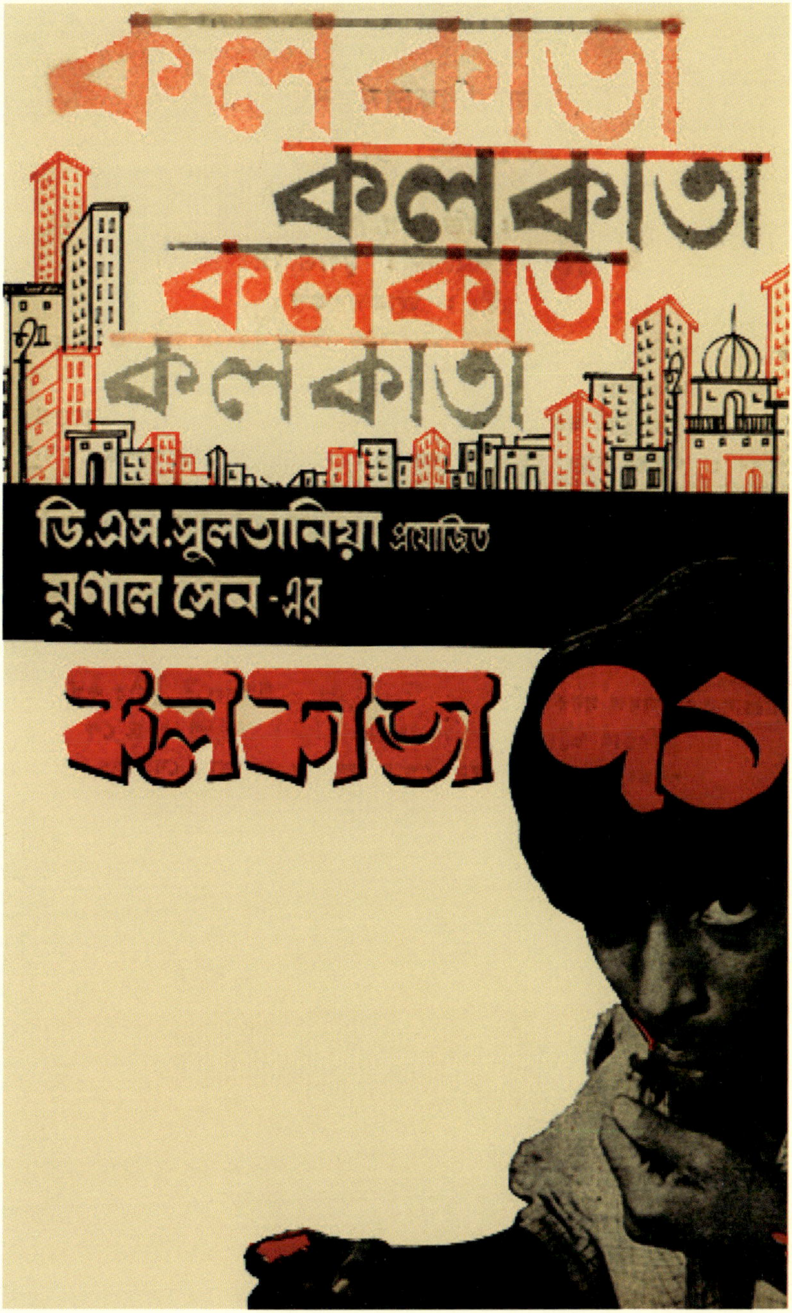
কলকাতা
কলকাতা
কলকাতা
কলকাতা
ডি.এস.সুলতানিয়া প্রযোজিত
মৃণাল সেন-এর
কলকাতা ৭১

মৃণাল সেনের
PADATiK

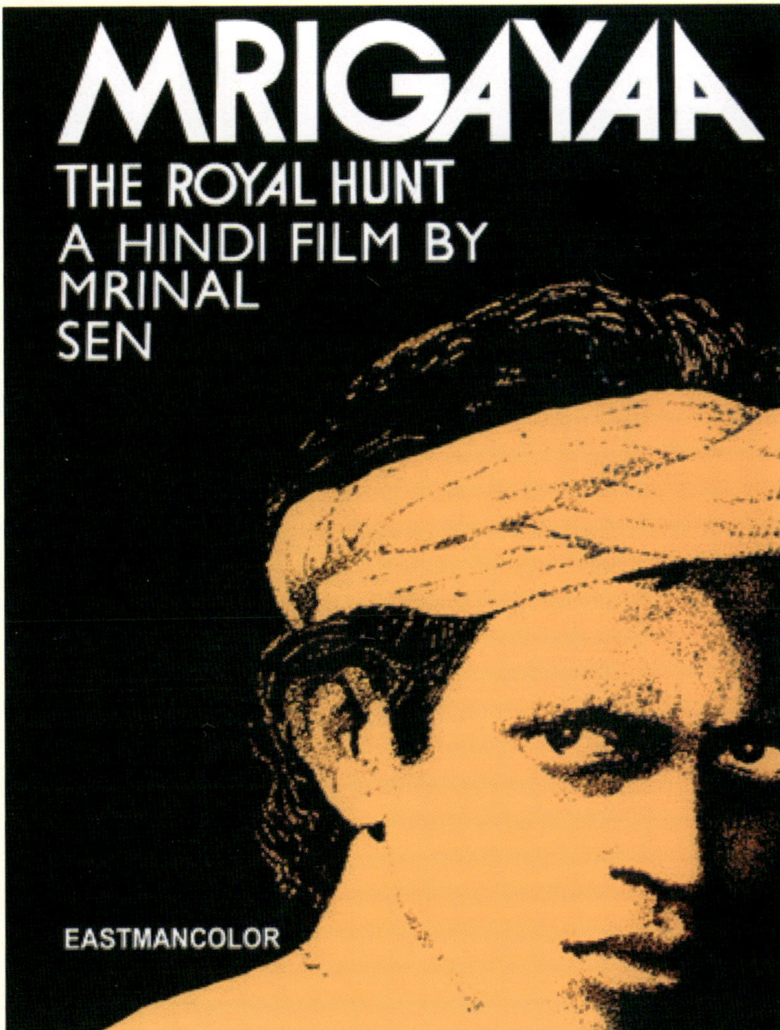
MRIGAYAA
THE ROYAL HUNT
A HINDI FILM BY
MRINAL
SEN
EASTMANCOLOR

MRINAL SEN'S

OKA OORIE KATHA

THE OUTSIDERS / LES MARGINAUX

PRODUCED BY CHANDRODAYA ART FILMS

মৃণাল সেনের
এক দিন প্রতিদিন
পরিবেশনাঃ ঊষা এন্টারপ্রাইজেস / ইস্টম্যানকালার

With wife Gita Sen

Directing Gita Sen in *Akaler Sandhane*

With film-maker Rituparno Ghosh during the shooting of *Aamaar Bhuvan*

The Sultans of the Seventies Arthouse – Mrinal Sen, Shyam Benegal and Satyajit Ray

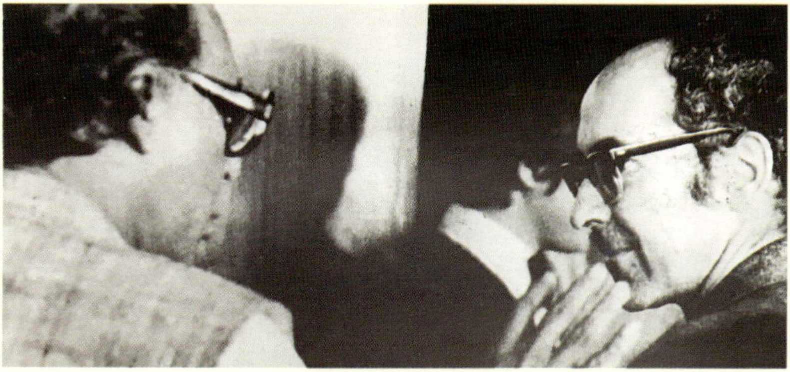

With Jean-Luc Godard

With Gabriel Garcia Marquez

With Satyajit Ray

Directing Smita Patil in *Akaler Sandhane*

Dimple Kapadia on the sets of *Antareen*

With Simi Garewal and cinematographer K.K. Mahajan, *Padatik*

With Dhritiman Chaterji on the sets of *Padatik*

On location, *Khandhar*

With Pt Ravi Shankar, music recording, *Genesis*

With K.K. Mahajan, *Chorus*

Lunch break on the sets of *Khandhar*

With Ranjit Mallick on the sets of *Interview*

On location, *Matira Manusha*

On location with Om Puri in *Genesis*

On location, *Bhuvan Shome*

Family time – with Gita, son Kunal and daughter-in-law Nisha

4

In His Own Words

Mrinal Sen passed into history on the morning of 30 December 2018. For me it was the end of nearly four decades of comradeship, the loss of a friend with whom I had spent hours of delectable adda. 'Adda' is a Bengali word that is difficult to translate—it encompasses everything from serious discussion to sheer gossip, from the exchange of thoughts to heated debates. Adda can be on any subject or can be without any subject at all and yet engrossing. Mrinal Sen had the quintessential adda personality. He was a conversationalist par excellence; he could talk on any subject tirelessly and could keep his listeners, young or old, spellbound for hours together.

My first exposure to this aspect of his personality was in 1979. I had recently been posted to the Directorate of Film Festival and was still finding my feet in the new office. On an autumn afternoon, Mrinal Sen just walked into my room, introduced himself and said he had brought with him the print of his latest film *Ek Din Pratidin*, and it had to be dispatched immediately to the Cannes Film Festival for preview, but he did not have a subtitled copy. That would be available a week later. I was shocked at his casual confidence—he dared to send an unsubtitled print to Cannes! Equally, I was awed by his personality. As we began to sort out the procedure for sending a second copy, I did remember to offer him a cup of coffee; he sat down, took out his packet of cigarettes, and conversation began with a few questions about my academic background and interest in films and spilled over to his own interest in literature and contemporary writing. That day he was in my office till it closed, i.e., 6 p.m. Within those three hours, the revered Mrinal Sen had become Mrinal-da, a friend.

That was my first encounter with Mrinal Sen, the brilliant conversationalist. The world knows Mrinal Sen as an exceptional film-maker, but people close to him will always remember him as the heart-throb of the quintessentially Bengali adda. With his two favourite stimulants—cups and cups of black tea and packets of cigarettes—he could literally speak for hours. Like a typical Bengali adda, the subjects he touched upon changed from cinema to literature, from history and politics to social studies, psychology and even jokes. Once while attending a film festival abroad, we were staying in the same hotel, and I had the privilege of listening to him from midnight to 3 a.m. for almost a fortnight regularly. He was approaching sixty, yet on the following morning he would be fresh and active, never showing any sign of fatigue. Such was his vitality.

After two decades of close friendship, and after my biography on Mrinal Sen had been published and acclaimed worldwide, All India Radio invited me to record a long interview with him for their archive. I thought it would be an excellent opportunity to record his off-the-cuff impressions in a proper and nuanced manner, so those thoughts could be preserved. Hesitantly, I raised the issue, but found Mrinal-da agreeing to the proposal immediately. At that time, I was posted in Delhi, and Mrinal-da had just been nominated to the Rajya Sabha. Barring a few hours in Parliament House, he was unoccupied, a luxury unimaginable in Calcutta. So, on a lazy autumn afternoon of 1999 at his Member of Parliament flat in Western Court, Janpath, we began our adda to record Mrinal-da's thoughts and impressions of anything he chose to speak about. My idea was to draw him out for some different, fresh and exciting insights into his life. Part of this adda was recorded in the studios of AIR Delhi, but most of it was sessions at different times in different houses where Mrinal-da and Gita Boudi lived.

The dialogue took time to pick up momentum. For AIR, I tried to give a formal structure to the adda, otherwise there was every chance of it becoming a meandering and rambling account. When these adda sessions continued beyond the AIR requirements, we moved from his MP quarters to his Beltala Road residence in Calcutta and picked up the threads whenever we found the time to meet. One day I told him, 'Sometime in the future I will publish these recordings so everyone can get a glimpse of the unknown Mrinal Sen.' He had a mischievous smile as he replied, 'Wait till I have passed into history.'

What I present now is a translation of the recordings of those adda sessions.

*

Dipankar: Mrinal-da, today we want to hear your story from you, your life, education and anything related to these two subjects. We won't follow a set pattern, because I want to hear you speak as you want to. I also know that you hate nostalgia, but for the sake of history, even if briefly, we have to look back at the past. So, I want you to start with your date and place of birth and other such mundane details.

Mrinal-da: Well, let me start with a mandatory warning—please do not ask my age. I was born many summers ago, but how many I don't wish to count. On every birthday, I get many congratulatory messages, and my standard reply to everyone is—thanks for remembering my birthdate, but please forget my year of birth. Because the year of birth makes me feel that I am growing too old. Mind you, this warning applies to you also.

Another warning, before we formally start, let me make one thing clear—for each session you must come prepared with a long list of questions. I shall try to answer all your queries, but later, I may come up with something diametrically opposite. I am an expert in this game. I also cannot promise that whatever I say will be the absolute truth and nothing but the truth. Now, what was the question?

Dipankar: I thought we should start with your date of birth, place of birth and some details about your childhood.

Mrinal-da: Okay. Just this once, I will tell you my year of birth. But don't ever repeat this question, agreed? I was born in the year 1923, the date was 14 May. I was born in Faridpur, a small town in present-day Bangladesh. Although a district town, Faridpur had a rural ambience. I spent the growing-up years of my life there.

Dipankar: Any particular childhood memory?

Mrinal-da: Not really. My childhood was not particularly exciting, but a few unusual things did happen, which, looking back, I now find interesting. Do you know who my first dentist was? Netaji Subhas Chandra, no less.

Mrinal-da laughs heartily, and I am, to say the least, amazed.

Dipankar: This certainly needs elaboration.

Mrinal-da: Faridpur was a politically sensitive place. At that time, the Indian National Congress, particularly its outfit in Bengal, was sharply divided between the moderates and the extremists. My father, a lawyer by profession, was very close to the extremist faction. In those days, Faridpur hosted many political meetings and conferences, and leaders from Calcutta would go there regularly. Faridpur was not too far from Calcutta, the distance could be covered in, say, six hours. Subhas Bose—he was still a dynamic young leader in the Congress, yet to become a national figure or Netaji—used to come to Faridpur frequently to organize political meetings. On one occasion, he was to come to our house for a discussion with the local organizers. It was a hot summer day, and I had a toothache. I was just a toddler then. When Bose came to our place, I was howling my heart out. He asked my mother what the problem was. When my mother told him about my toothache, he said, 'Ask him to suffer the pain for one more day. Day after tomorrow, I have to come to Faridpur again, I will bring him medicine.'

Dipankar: And did he remember to bring the medicine?

Mrinal-da: Yes, he did, in spite of his busy schedule, he remembered. He also found the time to give my mother detailed instructions on how to apply the medicine. She put one drop on my affected tooth, and it worked like a charm.

Dipankar: One drop was enough to cure your pain?

Mrinal-da: Not exactly. I got temporary relief. Ultimately, the tooth had to be pulled out. I think there was something wrong with the roots. But, I consider Bose to be my first dentist. I still remember reading the label, which said 'made in Germany'. Probably, his German connection started with me.

Dipankar: Do you remember any other politicians?

Mrinal-da: Bose was a frequent visitor to Faridpur. But his mentor, C.R. Das, better known as Deshbandhu, was also a familiar face in the township. Everyone used to talk about the inspiring lecture he gave during a convention, but that was in the year of my birth, and I have no direct knowledge about it. Another eminent politician who came to Faridpur for a political convention was Bipin Chandra Pal, part of the famous Lal-Bal-Pal trio. That was also before my time, but I had heard stories of the ruckus created in my family by that visit.

Dipankar: How so?

Mrinal-da: Pal came to address a political meeting. My parents accompanied him. In those days the practice was that every meeting must start with a song. The organizers had not planned for an inaugural song. My father, who was also on the organizing committee, asked my mother to sing, and she, the dutiful wife, obliged with a Tagore song. People clapped and Pal also praised her. But a few days later, my grandmother sternly asked my mother, 'I am hearing that you sang in a public meeting?' My mother, who was very proud of her achievement, did not think of hiding the fact, and she readily began to describe the occasion. She was immediately stopped and got a thorough tongue-lashing. Grandmother kept wailing—'How did you dare to sing in front of so many people! Have you heard of any other woman from a decent family singing in public? Only women of ill-repute do that!' She went on and on. My father, hearing grandmother shouting, appeared on the scene, but to my mother's great surprise, he did not utter a word or even clarify that it was his idea to make mother sing in public.

Dipankar: But all this is hearsay. It gives me an idea of the times. I want to know how *you* remember those growing-up years. Do you remember anything about the political life of that era?

Mrinal-da: Well, looking back I think I mostly remember many, many people, maybe one hundred, maybe even more, coming to our home in the dead of the night. My mother used to feed them. They were all armed revolutionaries. Ultimately, the police would catch hold of them, and then my father would defend them in court. I clearly remember the excitement when he managed to save some of them from the gallows.

Dipankar: That means your parents gave shelter to revolutionaries. Did the news not spread?

Mrinal-da: Of course everybody knew. The police raided our home frequently, but they found no evidence.

Dipankar: It seems your father was a well-known lawyer. Did he have a roaring practice?

Mrinal-da: All I can tell you is that we were neither rich nor poor. The reason for that is we had a very large family. I had many siblings, elder and younger.

Dipankar: Were you good in studies?

Mrinal-da: My parents thought I was a good student. My results were never brilliant nor were they mediocre. I liked studying, I learnt the joy of reading from my teachers. Basically, I was a good boy, my teachers liked me. I went to school in the morning, played football with friends in the evening, did my homework at night and read storybooks before going to bed. That was how I spent my childhood. At that age, everyone has some dreams. I was not an exception, but I can't remember those idyllic thoughts. Perhaps there was nothing to talk about.

Dipankar: But what about that story I have heard about you hitting a teacher on his head? Did you really crack the head of one of your schoolteachers?

Mrinal-da: (*Laughs loudly*) Highly exaggerated. I have already told you that Faridpur was a politically sensitive place. There was always a meeting or a rally to attend. Once, Dr Shyama Prasad Mookerji came to address a Hindu Mahasabha rally. During his speech, he lost his cool and abused Subhas Bose. Bose was a hero among the local people, so the rude comments about him led to pandemonium on the stage, followed by fisticuffs among the audience. In our school, we had a bald teacher who was an aggressive Hindu. He was among the audience, and I heard him speak very excitedly and abusively about Subhas. I was carrying an umbrella, and I just slammed it on his head. That was the only act of violence I have ever committed in my life.

Dipankar: Nobody caught you?

Mrinal-da: Who was watching me in that melee? Besides, I had such a goody-goody boy image in school. Even Mr Baldy never suspected me. The next day he came to school wearing a bandage on his head like a victory badge. Only I knew how he had got those injuries!

Though the political atmosphere heated up now and then, I had for the most part a very uneventful childhood. I went to school, played with friends, occasionally attended political meetings, but not with any serious interest, passed my examinations without any hiccups. You can say my growing-up years were by and large uneventful, unexciting. Finally, I came to the end of my schooldays. I passed my matriculation and intermediate examinations. Then my parents decided to send me to Calcutta to pursue higher studies.

Dipankar: Were you excited about going to Calcutta? What were your feelings about leaving home, friends…

Mrinal-da: The day before my departure, I felt very depressed. The very thought of leaving my home and family and the thought of spending years in an unknown land with total strangers was severely depressing. I went to my parents and asked them, 'In all these years, have you ever noticed some spark of genius in me?' They were somewhat embarrassed, because they had obviously never seen any genius in me but did not know how to tell me to my face. I assured them by quoting a very wise man who had observed that every child up to the age of ten was a genius. With those words, leaving my parents in a quandary about my genius, I started for Calcutta.

Dipankar: Before we start exploring your life in Calcutta as a student, let me clarify a few points. You have told me that your family believed in the ideology of the Congress.

Mrinal-da: Yes, of course.

Dipankar: But you are well known for your pro-left disposition. Does this mean that those years in Faridpur had no impact on your political thoughts later in life?

Mrinal-da: No, Faridpur did play a role in my life. I have told you my father was an extremist in the Congress. In later years, quite a few communist leaders came out of that extremist faction within the Congress. Had my father lived longer, he could have become one of them. Ah! I just remembered something interesting. May I tell you?

Dipankar: Of course. I have told you I am not going to follow any set pattern.

Mrinal-da: In 1923, Faridpur hosted the All Bengal Ryot Conference. C.R. Das presided over the conference, and my father was the chairman of the Reception Committee. His speech was printed and distributed. After many, many years, I found a copy of that speech and read it. I was pleasantly surprised to see how reverentially he had spoken about the Bolshevik Revolution of 1917 and how he saw it transform Russia. I do not think he was the only one; many other leaders and workers of the Congress thought along similar lines. I have the highest regard for Munshi Premchand, the noted writer. He is known as a Gandhian. But he wrote in one of his novels—'If somebody hits you, hit back. There is nothing great in stomaching insult, it is cowardice.' That does not sound very Gandhian, does it?

Dipankar: But was your father a Gandhian?

Mrinal-da: Yes, he was. In the 1930s, Gandhiji was arrested immediately upon his arrival in India, after attending the Round Table Conference in London. A countrywide general strike was called to protest the arrest. My father also did not attend court. The following day, the district magistrate called all the lawyers and wanted to know the reason for their absence. Others gave various excuses, but my father bluntly told the DM that he had boycotted court to protest against Gandhiji's arrest. The DM was not amused; he issued an order banning my father from legal practice for six months. My father went to Calcutta High Court to appeal against the order. Sarat Chandra Bose, the well-known barrister and Netaji's elder brother, appeared in court on his behalf. He won the appeal and resumed his practice within three months. This is an incident I vividly remember. You talked about my pro-left attitude. At Faridpur College, I joined the Students' Federation of India, a leftist organization, and became an active member.

Dipankar: If you allow me, Mrinal-da, I am tempted here to fast forward a little, as you people may say, take a jump cut—

Mrinal-da: Yes, of course. I hope you remember Godard's famous dictum: a film should have a beginning, a middle and an end, but not necessarily in the same order. I also believe in that. So, go ahead.

Dipankar: Many, many years after leaving Faridpur, in 1973, you made a film called *Padatik*. The film depicts a clash between two generations—a father, a conventional, middle-class Bengali, and a son, a Naxalite. My question is, how much, if at all, is the relationship in the film autobiographical?

Mrinal-da: I cannot give a definitive reply. It is true that I have used many personal experiences in that film. Generation gap or generation clash is a universal phenomenon, and my life was no exception. But *Padatik* has many layers that one cannot ignore. The Communist Party of India was banned just after Independence, so the party went underground. I had watched this battle against the Establishment from very close quarters. I had also seen how a wall can come up between a leader and a worker; I used this knowledge in that film. I feel our memories never die; they just change form and shape. Whenever some external event provokes me, something from inside just comes up. I do not know the process or how it happens, but believe me, it has happened with me so many times. *Padatik* is an example. My childhood memories, my experiences in Calcutta, so many things found a place in that film.

Dipankar: Allow me to rephrase my question. At the end of *Padatik*, the father-son duo, in spite of their differences, reach a point where they can understand and support each other. In real life, did you become that close to your father?

Mrinal-da: I think I reached that point. In 1941, when I was still in college, I was arrested and spent seven days in jail. Every day, people from the Special Branch came and interrogated me. The government had banned the Communist Party of India, and the party had gone underground. The allegation against me was that I was the link between the overground and the underground.

But this was hogwash, I was no such thing. After seven days, I came out on bail. At the jail gate, I found my father waiting for me. He had come all the way from Faridpur. Just imagine the situation, the whole world knew that I was a communist and in tandem with the party leadership. And my father, a diehard supporter and worker of the Indian National Congress, held my hand and said quietly, 'Keep it up.' He uttered just this one sentence and nothing more.

Dipankar: This once again reminds me of *Padatik*, where in the final sequence, the father tells the son, 'Be brave.' That is the end of the dialogue. But Mrinal-da, I have read somewhere that you were arrested even during your schooldays?

Mrinal-da: (*Smiles*) Oh that was a farce! I think I was in class III, when senior students took out an anti-government procession and we, the tinytots, followed them. We were told to shout 'Vande Mataram' and some anti-police slogans. We were shouting merrily when a group of policemen appeared on the scene. All the senior students immediately disappeared, and like Casabianca, I alone stood on the burning deck. The sepoys took me to the police station and made me stand before the officer-in-charge's desk. Then a constable brought canes of different sizes and put them on the desk. He also brought a thick rope. The OC told me, 'Do you understand what these mean? We will hang you from this rope and cane you.' I started crying my heart out, but he continued to terrorize me. In the midst of this drama, my family members got the news and rushed to the police station. I think I was in police custody for about three hours—I am not sure whether it can be called an arrest.

Dipankar: Any more arrests in your life?

Mrinal-da: Yes, one more, ten years after the college incident, in 1951.

Dipankar: What was the issue this time?

Mrinal-da: Well, there was really no issue. This was the time we were desperately trying to make a film.

Dipankar: 'We' means?

Mrinal-da: Me and my four friends—Ritwik Ghatak, Salil Choudhury, Kali Banerjee and Tapas Sen. By then, we knew all about the film movements in France and Italy. Every day, for hours together, we would discuss aspects of making meaningful cinema while sitting at a small teashop, Paradise Café, in Kalighat. We did not even have the money to pay for tea, but the shopowner had a soft corner in his heart for us. He would send to our table a big mugful of tea and some empty cups. One day, I was walking towards the café when I noticed a commotion, people running in the street in a desperate kind of way. Before I realized what was happening, two constables grabbed me and dumped me inside a black van. Later I came to know that two minutes before I had arrived on the spot, a bomb had exploded in the nearby Kalighat tram depot. The police were looking for the arsonist when they encountered me walking casually by.

Dipankar: How was the experience this time?

Mrinal-da: Oh, that time the police action was terrible. They took me to the police station, where they searched me thoroughly. Of course, they found nothing, no money nor anything incriminating. But there was a piece of paper in my pocket on which I had noted down some points from a book by Ralph Fox. Have you heard of him?

Dipankar: No, I don't think I have heard the name.

Mrinal-da: He was a fairly important author of our times. He had joined the Spanish Civil War as part of the International Brigade and died in action there. His *The Novel and the People* was quite famous. The policeman took the paper and asked me, 'What is this?' I replied, 'Notes from a book called *The Novel and the People.*' The policeman sneered, 'So, you read English novels and also hurl bombs?' I replied, 'How do you know that I throw bombs?' The policeman shouted at me—'Otherwise, why would they arrest you?' The interrogation went on like that—the police trying to pin me down to admitting that I knew about the bomb while I kept telling them I had nothing to do with any such activity.

Dipankar: Any third-degree treatment?

Mrinal-da: Not exactly, but there were lots of pushes and prods. An officer called me for interrogation; he was sitting at a table with an empty chair on the other side. I drew up the chair and tried to sit, but a constable shoved me hard and said, 'Stand up.' I told the officer, 'Your man is assaulting me before you and you are not saying anything to him.' The officer ignored my remark and started asking questions. It began with—'What is your name? What is the name of your father?' and continued in a singsong manner. Many years later, I used some of that experience in the police station sequence in my film, *Interview*. Do you remember?

Dipankar: Yes, I do. But we will have to travel a long way to reach that point. Now, we will go to Calcutta with you. You have just stepped down on the platform of Sealdah station. You are seventeen and a half, maximum eighteen. Am I right?

Mrinal-da: Yes, you are.

Dipankar: What next?

Mrinal-da: It was a strange experience. From a half-village, half-town, I had just gatecrashed into a metropolis without any preparation, without any idea of what a big city can be like. At the railway station itself, I encountered a huge crowd, a conglomeration of faceless, nameless humanity, none of whom I knew. This was unimaginable at Faridpur, where I knew everyone. I felt a strange void and felt like an outsider.

Dipankar: But now you proudly proclaim that you are a genuine, 100 per cent Calcuttan. How did this happen? I want to hear about the process that made the outsider an insider.

Mrinal-da: Let us start with Mrinal in Calcutta in our next session. There is much too much to tell, some of which I need to recollect in my mind.

Calcutta: My El Dorado

Dipankar: We will begin with your first thoughts about the young man who felt himself an outsider among a sea of unknown faces…

Mrinal-da: Looking back, I now feel I went a bit overboard with my loneliness. Perhaps there were too many 'firsts'; eating with a bunch of total strangers was a novel experience and so was paying for your meals. During my first community meal, I made a mess. I still remember it vividly. We had sat down for a meal in my lodge, they gave me a slice of lemon to mix its juice with my rice and daal, I probably squeezed it too hard, and the lemon slipped out of my hand and landed on another man's plate. I was awfully embarrassed, and the stranger on whose plate it had landed gave me a stern look. He did not smile; did not say a word to me, but with a straight face, he just asked the cook to change the plate.

Dipankar: A typical Calcutta scene in a lodge! You should have used it in one of your films. Did you later become friendly with your co-boarders?

Mrinal-da: Not really, because I preferred to spend time with my political fellow-travellers. I have told you that I got involved in student politics in my Faridpur days. I even became the secretary of the district's Students' Federation. I continued that association in Calcutta, though that old fervour was no more. It was compulsory for us to attend a special class on Marxism conducted by senior leaders like Biswanath Mukherjee. One day a senior called me and showed me a note. In that note, Biswanath babu had written, 'Mrinal Sen does not attend class and even if he attends, he does not apply his mind. You must talk to him and convince him that he must be more attentive in future. I think the boy has potential.' The senior who showed me the note thought I would be repentant and embarrassed; instead, to his utter surprise and horror, I jumped with joy. I was in seventh heaven. It was beyond my wildest dreams that a leader of Biswanath babu's stature would take a personal interest in my activities and would be so confident about my potential.

Dipankar: Did you rise up to the occasion and fulfil his expectations?

Mrinal-da: No, because I never became a member of the party. I was close with various leftist political organizations and worked with them even when those parties were banned. But I refused to be a card-carrying member because that would bind me to the discipline of the party and affect my personal life. After some years, a prominent leftist leader tried to pressure me to join his party. I told him, 'Look, joining your party means if I want to be chummy with a pretty woman, I have to take your permission. That is not possible. I am not ready to accept anybody's moral guardianship.' Don't be under the misconception that I wanted to be a Casanova. Nor did I move around with many girls. I was friendly with only one sweet girl who subsequently became my wife.

Dipankar: But you did fall in love with Calcutta. The various ways in which you have presented Calcutta in your films is unique. I don't think any other film-maker has done it. What is the reason behind this strange attraction?

Mrinal-da: I cannot talk about others. But I started loving Calcutta slowly, gradually and unknowingly. Slowly it dawned on me that I could not live without loving this city. That was when I started proclaiming that Calcutta was my El Dorado. In this connection, I would like to recall the experience of a famous foreign film-maker in Calcutta.

Dipankar: Foreign film-maker?

Mrinal-da: Louis Malle, the well-known French director. Surely you have heard his name.

Dipankar: I think many years ago he made a film on Calcutta, which became controversial.

Mrinal-da: I found nothing objectionable in the film, but I did not like it either. Anyway, let me continue with my story. It was the latter half of 1968; Calcutta was bursting with excitement and protests. Every afternoon, there was an anti-government rally or demonstration, one day by students, another day by peasants, the next day it could be by some women's organizations or some other group. About the same time, I had somehow organized some money to hire a 35mm movie camera and raw stock; whenever there was a clash between the police and the agitators, I tried to reach the spot and record everything. It was not a great work of art, but no other film-maker in the country had thought about doing it.

Dipankar: Did you begin to plan your Calcutta trilogy from the late sixties?

Mrinal-da: No, not exactly. But I vaguely thought of utilizing the footage in my forthcoming productions.

Dipankar: But how did Louis Malle figure in this?

Mrinal-da: Malle had first visited Calcutta the previous winter, as a member of a French film delegation. That was how I met him. I also interviewed him for All India Radio. We became quite friendly. The next year, I got a phone call from him. 'Mrinal, I am in Calcutta with my cameraman and sound recordist. I am shooting a film on the crowds on Calcutta's streets.' I replied, 'My God, don't you know what is happening here? The city is on the boil. Every day there are demonstrations on the streets. Even today there is a massive protest rally where two hundred thousand students will stage a civil disobedience and break laws.' I could almost see Malle dancing with excitement as he replied, 'Two hundred thousand! In one spot! I covered the rallies in Sorbonne early this year, but this is out of this world! Mrinal, I must have this.' But I had to disappoint him—'Sorry Louis, you won't be allowed to shoot these rallies. That is the law of the land.' He protested—'What do you mean, why can't I shoot? I have written permission from Delhi.' I explained to him, 'If you carefully read through that piece of paper you will find somewhere in fine print that, as a foreigner, you are not supposed to shoot anything political.' He was crestfallen. I told him, 'Let's see if I can find a way to help you.'

Dipankar: So, you decided to find loopholes in our law and encouraged a foreigner to break the law along with the students.

Mrinal-da: Don't jump to the wrong conclusion hastily; the real story starts here. Malle promptly arrived at my house and we reached the site of the rally well in advance. Meanwhile, I had contacted some student leaders to turn up in full strength. Keeping Malle and his team sitting in the car, I came out to watch the police reaction to the student congregation. I did not have to wait long.

Soon a police jeep screeched in, and a deputy commissioner of police stepped out. I knew him a little. So, I went up to him and asked very innocently, 'So, you are today's commander-in-chief?'

He replied with a grim face, 'Unfortunately, yes.'

I made a request to him—'I want to record a part of the demonstrations, please help me select a good angle.'

He did not care much about a camera following the police action or the demonstrating students and casually replied, 'You can select your angle, nobody will stop you.'

Then I tried to be a little more demanding and said, 'Thank you, but I have one more request. A foreign friend of mine has come from France with his camera team…'

Even before I could complete the sentence he sternly told me, 'Sorry, Mrinal babu, that I can't allow. My hands are tied.'

I pleaded—'But he is an internationally acclaimed film-maker from France, and he loves the city. He will show nothing damaging.'

The deputy commissioner suddenly became quite excited and asked, 'French film-maker? Who is he?'

I replied, 'Louis Malle.'

Now he could not suppress his eagerness. 'Is Louis Malle in town? Mrinal babu, I must meet him.'

So, I asked Louis to come out of the car and duly introduced him. The DCP said, 'Only last week, I watched your film at the Alliance Française and I loved it.'

I was very surprised and asked him, 'Was it an English subtitled print?'

The DCP said, 'No, but language wasn't a problem for me. You see, I have a diploma in French, I have translated Aragon's poems into Bengali,' and then he started reciting French poetry. So, everything was settled amicably.

Malle drew me aside and said, 'Mrinal, I am overwhelmed. This cannot happen anywhere else in the world. This bloody policeman will beat up these innocent boys savagely, but the same bloke watches my films, reads poetry—I just can't imagine it. This happens only in Calcutta.'

Dipankar: Louis Malle is right, such things happen only in Calcutta. But Mrinal-da, we still do not know what happened with you in Calcutta. You came here for higher studies—what about that?

Mrinal-da: I got admission in Scottish Church College, one of the well-known institutions in the city. I took up an honours course in physics. I liked the college. Even in 1940, that college was a co-educational institution.

Dipankar: So, how did your relationship with Calcutta progress?

Mrinal-da: Well, it was a multifaceted one. It was overtly political—I have already told you about my arrest. But there was a great churning in the cultural field also. The Indian People's Theatre Association was born around that time.

Dipankar: Did you become a member of the IPTA?

Mrinal-da: No, I have already clarified that I was never a card-carrying member of any organization. In Calcutta, the IPTA movement was spearheaded by stalwarts like Shombhu Mitra and Bijan Bhattacharya. Even writers and critics like Sudhi Pradhan and Gopal Haldar would occasionally put on grease paint and appear on stage. I was fascinated by those performances as they introduced a new aesthetic. Soon IPTA began to dominate the cultural scene in the city.

Dipankar: They inspired you to become a film-maker?

Mrinal-da: Not really. At that time I never thought about becoming a film-maker. I was not even particularly fond of cinema. Like any young man of my age, I would occasionally watch a film. That was also the era when I experienced many things, and all those experiences were not as pleasant as the dramas I saw on stage.

Dipankar: The turbulent forties? Or the impact of the Second World War?

Mrinal-da: I am talking about the Great Bengal Famine of 1943. At least a million people of undivided Bengal literally starved to death. Lakhs of men, women and children from villages rushed to the Big City, looking for a mouthful of food. But even in Calcutta, who would give them food? All they asked for was some starch, nothing more, and they did not even get that. Every day, as I walked on the streets of Calcutta, I could see corpses scattered on the pavement, on the roadside. That was the way ten lakh people died. Then I also saw the follow-up.

Dipankar: You mean, the Great Calcutta Killing, the Partition and Independence.

Mrinal-da: Yes, all those and more. For the country, it was the worst of times, but for me, it was the best of times. I think I am sounding too Dickensian. But those incidents taught me many things, and most importantly, they made me familiar with a bigger world. In 1937, I had followed the Spanish Civil War, where the international brigade of intellectuals fought against the Franco regime and lost. Ten years later, I saw how we led ourselves to accept the Partition and the transfer of power.

Dipankar: How much did the Partition affect your family in Faridpur?

Mrinal-da: Some of my elder brothers had already moved to Calcutta; my parents followed them around 1948. My father had wanted to remain in Faridpur, but the circumstances were not favourable. He probably felt lonely there. Around this time, something significant happened to me. A politician friend of my father from the Congress had become influential in the new regime. He called me over and suggested, 'Why don't you register as a refugee with the state government? I can help you get regular dole, you can even get financial assistance to start a business.' Something inside me refused to accept the word 'refugee' written next to my father's name. I bluntly told him, 'No thanks. I have been living in this city since 1941, I am not a refugee, nor shall I become one.'

Dipankar: You took a very bold stand especially given that times were so difficult.

Mrinal-da: But that is my relationship with Calcutta. To me, Calcutta is like a woman whom I love and hate at the same time. This city had already given me a lot; it introduced me to the bigger world. I would never be a refugee in this city. I would have liked to call myself a citizen of the world like Chaplin, but how can I forget Calcutta?

Dipankar: The same city where you were told to register as a refugee gave you a civic reception some time ago. How did you feel about that?

Mrinal-da: It was a moment of great pride and joy. It was a rare moment of happiness to be honoured by the mayor of Calcutta. But I was happy mostly because on that day I could finally convince my wife for the first time in our life that I had achieved some eminence; she was now the wife of a VIP. It is really difficult for any man to be a VIP for his wife.

Dipankar: While listening to your reminiscences of those pre-Independence days, one thing strikes me. The famine really shook you up badly, which is why it comes back in your films regularly, from *Baishey Shravana* to *Akaler Sandhane*—

Mrinal-da: And there was *Calcutta 71* in between.

Dipankar: Exactly. My question is, why did you not make a film on communal riots and the Partition of India? In this context, the name of Ritwik Ghatak comes up inevitably. But even without taking anyone's name, did this subject not inspire or provoke you enough?

Mrinal-da: This requires a long answer. Let us take up famine first. I never forgot the famine of 1943, but it was not possible for me to rebuild the Calcutta of 1943. So, what was my choice? Take *Calcutta 71*. A young man tells the audience, 'I am twenty, for the last thousand-odd years. During this long period, I have walked mile after mile, trampling through poverty, dirt and death. I want to tell you that our history is the history of exploitation and poverty.' Then the film starts. The first story is of 1933, written by Manik Bandopadhyay—the theme is poverty. After that episode is over, the youth comes back and repeats,

'I am twenty', etc., etc. The next story is of 1943, written by Prabodh Kumar Sanyal. Here also the theme is poverty and exploitation, but the mood is totally different. This is followed by a Samaresh Basu story of 1953, dealing with a totally different class of people, but the theme remains the same. Finally, we come to 1971. Time has changed but not the face of poverty. That is symbolized by the icon of the fasting Buddha of the Gandhara era, where you can count almost all the bones of his body. In 1971, the poor villager who is squatting on the pavement of Calcutta has a similar skeletal look. Two and a half thousand years have passed by but the face of poverty has remained unchanged.

Dipankar: The same Buddha icon you used again in *Akaler Sandhane*.

Mrinal-da: Yes. But remember, I created an atmosphere of famine mainly through stills. It is extremely difficult to recreate the Calcutta of 1943 today. If I really wanted to depict the Calcutta of 1943, I would have had to take the floor space of at least three studios and build a set there. That was way beyond my means. Besides, I did not want to recreate the horror, I just wanted the audience to feel what poverty can be. I procured those stills from the archives of *The Statesman* and other newspapers. I thought even those stills provided a sense of mobility. But my critics screamed—these are Mrinal Sen's gimmicks. Sorry, I think I am going beyond the range of your question—

Dipankar: Please carry on, I think these points are relevant.

Mrinal-da: But who can decide what a gimmick is. Shakespeare writes the entire play *Julius Caesar* in English but just adds 'et tu, Brute', which he could have written in English, but did not. Is that a gimmick? No, because that adds a new dimension to his agony. Do you understand?

Dipankar: Let us return to famine. Your point is that without presenting the physicality of the famine, your emphasis is on its inherent ugliness. Am I right?

Mrinal-da: Absolutely. Let us go back to *Baishey Shravana*. I never tried to say how many lives were lost. I only showed how a man loses his humanity, his decency. My camera did not capture the ugly face of famine; I only showed how a man loses his values if he is deprived of food. Now I return to your main question, why I never made a film on the Partition.

The Partition happened in 1947. But even before that, I saw the plight of the Burmese refugees, who had lost their hearth and home because of the Japanese occupation. I also volunteered to provide relief to them. Personally, I was not very affected by the Partition, but I spent days in refugee colonies, helping them in different ways. I had seen films made on this subject, like Nemai Ghosh's *Chinnamul*, and realized how powerful the medium of cinema could be. Nemai Ghosh was not a great film director, you can question the quality or standard of his film-making, but the honesty and integrity of the film-maker was beyond doubt. You just commented that Ritwik made films on Partition, but is that really so? Nemai Ghosh's film showed how refugees jumped on the platform from running trains; you won't find such visuals in Ritwik's movies. Ritwik's subject is not the Partition but people who lost everything, including their roots and their misery.

Dipankar: You have opened a new line of thought. I never looked at it from this angle.

Mrinal-da: A very powerful work on communal riots is Govind Nihalani's *Tamas*, made for television. Another excellent film, although slightly limited in range, is M.S. Sathyu's *Garam Hawa*. I would have been very happy to make such a film, but honestly speaking, I have never tried. I am more interested in depicting an individual's problems than in upheaval within a community or in recreating the past.

Dipankar: We have gone through the first twenty-five years of your life. By that time, your tastes, mood and attitudes were set. Shall we now proceed to your passion for cinema?

Cinema and Other Passions

Dipankar: When did you watch your first film? Do you remember the film?

Mrinal-da: Well, the first film I watched was in Faridpur, at a very, very tender age. Only during annual festivals, when the travelling cinema came to town, did we get to see a few films. My parents and family members, the neighbourhood, all of us went together to watch those films. I too was taken to enjoy the novelty. Faridpur had no proper cinema hall; films were screened in tents. I would watch the film-screenings with awe. I remember myself watching the moving images, wide-eyed and open-mouthed; the wonder of moving pictures lingered in my mind. I must have seen many films, but I distinctly remember three—*Devdas, Kapalkundala* and *The Kid*—what a queer combination.

Dipankar: *Devdas*? You mean the Pramathesh Barua-starrer?

Mrinal-da: No, no, it was an earlier, silent version. But, I still remember something interesting in that movie. An adolescent Devdas climbs up a mango tree to pinch a few fruits, while a young Parvati watches from below. Suddenly, a guard comes up with a big stick, forcing Devdas to come down. At that point it starts raining in the film. I was so absorbed in the film that I did not realize that outside the tent it had started to rain as well, and the sound of raindrops hitting the tin roof was real! Soon the reel rain and real rain blended perfectly. What a wonderful coincidence! Now, I know that happened accidentally, but when I started thinking about cinema seriously, I realized even at that tender age the importance of blending the visual with the audio in cinema. This experience has helped me throughout my career. I was barely seven or eight then.

Dipankar: When did you first consider the prospect of becoming a film-maker?

Mrinal-da: To be perfectly frank and to confess unabashedly, I initially had no interest in cinema. Even when I came to Calcutta, I failed to become an addict. I saw a few films, but I was not a regular filmgoer. I have already told you about my IPTA days. I never missed their shows. Those were the days of war, famine, riot, Partition and Hiroshima and Nagasaki going up in flames. All those and other situations in a society ruled by colonial masters and their native lackeys found a place in those shows—IPTA staged *Nabanna* (Harvest), *Ram Lila*. These were the biggest draws among all classes of people. That was why I, never a participant, decided at some point in the mid-forties that I would like to showcase reality. That was how I began to think that I too should be in show business!

Dipankar: How did you prepare yourself for this role?

Mrinal-da: As a student of physics, I was fascinated by the science of sound. So, I thought of learning sound recording. In those days, the best sound recordist in town was Sambhu Singh, a Sikh who spoke flawless Bengali.

He worked in Aurora Studios, so I approached the studio owner, Anadi Nath Bose. He knew my father, so he agreed to accommodate me for three months so I could learn the ropes of sound recording. For the next couple of months, I worked as an unpaid apprentice to Sambhu Singh to learn the absolute basics of sound recording.

Dipankar: Since you were attached to a studio, did you watch any shooting of films?

Mrinal-da: Trust me, I never did. Although lots of things were happening around Aurora. Ajay Bhattacharya, the well-known lyricist, was directing a movie with Chhabi Biswas as the hero, but I honestly never felt like visiting the sets. After two months, I was bored with handling the sound recording machines, so I stopped going there. This, you can say, was the end of Chapter I.

Dipankar: How and when did Chapter II start?

Mrinal-da: In the most unlikely place—at the Imperial Library, which is now called the National Library. The year was 1943 or '44. I had duly graduated but had no regular job, nor any prospect of getting employment in the foreseeable future. So, to keep myself engaged, I began to visit the library and spent my time reading. Soon it became a regular habit—I would reach the library at nine sharp in the morning, read books the whole day and leave at closing time in the evening. This routine continued for months together.

Dipankar: But what did you read?

Mrinal-da: Anything and everything. I did not bother about academic discipline. I enjoyed reading books—my preference was for literature, sociology and philosophy. I still remember I read Firdausi's *Shahnama*, a monumental work in fourteen volumes. In that reading room, I discovered the works of a Czech writer, whose name nobody had heard in our country. He was Karel Capek. I first read his play, *Mother*, which I liked. Then I picked up his last novel, published posthumously, and I liked it so much that I started translating it into Bengali in the library itself. This became my first published work.

Dipankar: Very interesting. What was the title of your book?

Mrinal-da: Capek called his book *The Cheat*. I did not change the title. It was published as *Cheat*.

Dipankar: What else did you read?

Mrinal-da: Many things. I read a bit of Lenin and Marx. Then I read Matthew Arnold's essays and Nietzsche's *Thus Spake Zarathustra*. Now you know how unfocussed and haphazard my reading was. One day, I discovered a book called *Film*. Just *Film*. I still remember the author's name. It was Rudolf Arnheim. A book published around 1934 or '35.

Dipankar: Was he an assistant to Eisenstein?

Mrinal-da: No, that was another Arnheim. He wrote on the aesthetics of different art forms; film was one of those disciplines. I was overwhelmed by the book, although I understood only half of it as it was full of references to various masterpieces, and I had no knowledge about those films. There was no film society in those days, so how could I have knowledge about European cinema? I only realized that cinema was a powerful medium of art. Thus started my love affair with cinema.

Dipankar: How did the affair proceed?

Mrinal-da: The day after I finished reading Arnheim's book, I was the first visitor to the library. I went through the catalogue, looking for books on cinema. This time, I got *The Cinema as a Graphic Art* by Vladimir Nilsen, who was a student of Eisenstein. A large part of the book was devoted to how Eisenstein used to teach. I did not fully understand this book either, but it genuinely attracted me. It also dealt with make-up, costumes. I paid lots of attention to those details, so I still remember them. In this way, I read up everything on cinema that the library had, and that was a lot. Then I started collecting books on cinema.

Dipankar: But this was entirely academic.

Mrinal-da: Yes, but those books changed my interest in cinema. From reading to becoming a film-lover was an equally difficult journey. The more I read, the more I felt the need to actually see some films. So I became a regular moviegoer. I mostly watched Bengali and Hindi movies. Most of them were atrocious, and I developed a strong hatred for bad cinema. Slowly I switched to foreign films, especially European films.

Dipankar: Where did you see those films? Was it through Film Society screenings?

Mrinal-da: Not really. The Calcutta Film Society was born in 1948. Much before that I watched films at different consulates. I managed invitations by writing about cinema in magazines. I wrote on all aspects of cinema—cinema and literature, cinema and music—in short, the aesthetics of cinema became my subject. Writing also helped expand my horizon.

Dipankar: Did you write your book on Chaplin then?

Mrinal-da: No, that was much later, that book came out in 1951. But first I must talk about my growing interest in films. If you want to discover me from our chat sessions, you have to hear me out.

Dipankar: Yes, we must know how a self-taught film-maker like you trained yourself before taking the fateful plunge.

Mrinal-da: Well, my fellow traveller in this journey was Ritwik Ghatak. He was already assisting Nirmal Dey, a well-known film-maker of that era. One of Ritwik's brothers went to Germany to learn cinematography. That was how he drifted to cinema. He also used to study a bit. Another friend was Hrishikesh Mukherjee, who was already working with New Theatres for the princely salary of Rs 60 per month. He was the richest among us and felt a bit vulnerable before us because he could not find the time to read about cinema and often had to sit quietly and listen to our exchange of ideas during adda sessions. But he was a great friend; he helped us financially too.

Dipankar: Was it out of compassion or a sense of duty?

Mrinal-da: Not compassion, he knew he was the weak link in our adda. And he wanted to do something to be an equal. Then, there was Tapas Sen, who was already providing lights for various stage productions. He too financed us. We somehow had the conviction that the day would soon come when all of us would enter the world of cinema. This was what we passionately discussed at the Paradise Café—I have already spoken about the place.

Dipankar: You still had no job, no regular source of income. How did you manage financially?

Mrinal-da: Pretty badly, I must admit. My earnings from writing were meagre, and I had to fall back on private tuition. Ritwik was not that hard-pressed, he constantly borrowed from his brothers—his brothers were well off.

Dipankar: After the Partition, you must have had various other problems too.

Mrinal-da: Yes, problems galore. I took up translation work and for some time got a job as a proofreader in a reputed publishing house. But they were unhappy if I corrected anything other than spelling mistakes. I, on the other hand, wanted to make changes to the text. Soon enough I knew this would not last long and began to search for another job. That was how I landed myself the job of a medical representative without knowing anything about medicines. The headquarters of the medical firm was in Kanpur, and I was posted there. By then, Ritwik had managed a job in the story department of Filmistan. One of his uncles had helped him. Another friend in our group, Salil Choudhury, had joined Bimal Roy Productions in Bombay. So, our entire Paradise Café group, with the solitary exception of Tapas (Sen), left Calcutta.

Dipankar: Did you like Kanpur?

Mrinal-da: Initially it was fine. I had some money in hand, and the work was simple. I was supposed to meet various doctors in the city regularly and sing the praises of the medicines manufactured by my company. I visited the doctors, chatted with them about anything and everything, but never spoke about the medicines. That was probably why most of the doctors liked me, and I became quite popular among the medical fraternity. The management was happy, and after six months I was transferred back to Calcutta.

Dipankar: But you gave up the job after coming to Calcutta?

Mrinal-da: Actually, I was getting bored with my profession. Often, I pretended to go on doctors' visits but did not go. I even sent concocted reports to the headquarters that I had met so-and-so. But soon enough word got around that I was not working as per orders. Even some of the doctors complained to the company that their representative had not visited them for a long time. The management was furious and transferred me back to Kanpur. Something else was keeping me more occupied—I was madly in love; my parents had liked the girl and wanted me to marry her. I wasn't sure if that was the right time to marry, but I needed to stay in Calcutta, be near my girlfriend. So, I tried to buy time by going on long leave without pay; in the process, I became dead broke and had no idea how I could continue to stay in Calcutta, earn some money, get into the film world like my friends. It was a peculiar situation—like a tunnel without end.

Dipankar: Why didn't you try some other job?

Mrinal-da: Well, I did get an offer. A teaching job at a school in a remote village in Hooghly district. Boarding and lodging was free at a villager's home in exchange for free tuition to his children. The salary was not bad considering the times—I think I was offered Rs 50, or maybe even Rs 60. The headmaster of the school came down to Calcutta to interview me. He approved my candidature and even paid me Rs 10 as advance travelling allowance. The route was by train up to Arambagh and the remaining part by bullock cart. Everything was finalized, but in the end I did not make it.

Dipankar: What went wrong?

Mrinal-da: I had another adda group at Kamalalaya, a big department store on Dharmatala Street in Central Calcutta. It had a book section, and I knew the store in-charge quite well. He would loan me brand-new books for two or three days. In this section, every evening, a select group of intellectuals would gather for sheer adda—they were all very senior and reputed people such as the author Gopal Haldar, the academician Professor Niren Roy. I was an insignificant nobody among them, but they had great affection for me. They had encouraged me to go to Kanpur, but when they heard about the Arambagh job, these veterans insisted that I must not run away to a godforsaken village to teach village kids but should build my future in Calcutta. I too liked the idea, and so I stayed put.

Dipankar: But what did you do? Did they offer you a job?

Mrinal-da: No, no, they only gave me vocal stimulus and the confidence to stay in Calcutta and try my luck. I, on the other hand, found all avenues of earning closed, and suddenly I decided to make a film. It was like a last choice.

Dipankar: How did your family react? In the mid-1940s, planning to make a film was not a very acceptable proposition.

Mrinal-da: My family had virtually given up on me. My father did warn me that if I took up film-making as a profession, it would be impossible to marry me to a girl from a decent family. At that time, neither of us knew that a decent girl would fall in love with me. My wife Gita came from a poor family, she lived in Uttarpara, and she became an actress to run the household. I first met her in the studio. I used to discuss politics with her and gifted her books to broaden her horizons.

Dipankar: I have heard from old-timers of Tollygunge that she was the heroine and you the assistant director of a film. That was how the romance bloomed. Is this story true? Was there such a film?

Mrinal-da: Yes, but it remained unfinished, and thank God for that, otherwise it was bound to have been a horrible movie. But since you mentioned romance, let me tell you a story. Once, I was visiting Uttarpara to meet Gita. Before boarding the train, I bought a cheap paperback from the station bookstall. The book was *The Case for Communism*, written by William Gallacher, the last communist MP in the British Parliament. While returning in the evening, we were walking down the massive bridge on the Ganga. It was a very romantic set-up, with the sun going down and the water splashing on the pillars and not a soul around us. We had never been intimate before, but that day I felt like kissing her. But I was so nervous that my lips landed on her nose and from my trembling hands, *The Case for Communism* fell into the river. With my first kiss, Gallacher's arguments for communism floated silently into the sea and were washed away from my mind.

Dipankar: Wonderful sequence and symbolic too. So, you faced no opposition to your marriage plans.

Mrinal-da: Both my parents liked Gita tremendously, and the marriage was organized very quickly. In fact, I still do not know why I was in such a tremendous hurry to marry. I had neither money, nor a job—it was the bleakest period of my life. I just lived, clinging to the hope that something would turn up.

Dipankar: And when did that happen?

Mrinal-da: Around 1954, a well-known actress of Calcutta, out of the blue, asked me to direct a film that she wanted to produce. She also made it clear that she would not act in the movie. She was a fine lady from an aristocratic family. She came to know of me from my writings. She somehow organized a meeting and immediately offered me the opportunity to make a film! And that was how I ultimately became a film-maker. My parents were happy that at last, I was settled in my life. My father passed away before the film was ready, which was a blessing in disguise because had he seen the film, he would have had a massive heart attack. I have not seen a more atrocious and ugly film in my life.

Dipankar: I know, you always become agitated whenever the subject of your debut film comes up. We will come back to it in due course. Let us now look at some of the themes of your cinema.

My Cinema, My Concepts about the Language of Films

Dipankar: We are now going to explore your life as a film-maker. But we will not move chronologically, perhaps we can fast forward a little and then come back to your initial years. I would like you to talk about a film you made in the mid-1960s, a film not particularly well-known or much watched. It is called *Matira Manisha*, made in Odia. In this film the protagonist is the youngest son of the family. He is a good-for-nothing chap with no job or income, but he gets married, and the film centres on the problems his wife has in adjusting with the rest of the family. Would you call the film autobiographical?

Mrinal-da: Before I answer your question, I must tell you about a dream I regularly had during my childhood. I used to dream that in the dead of the night, the mythological Garuda was flying around my home. After a few rounds, he would enter my room through the window and tell me, 'Come on, I will give you a ride.' I would promptly jump on his back; he would fly me around and after a few rounds, Garuda would drop me on my bed. I had this dream many times, and I used this imagery in the film *Matira Manisha*.

Dipankar: Have you tried to analyse this dream?

Mrinal-da: I think one particular childhood memory is at the root of this dream. When I was just a toddler, I saw an airplane for the first time. I still remember that the plane came down very low and then flew high up in the sky, and the whole town burst into excitement. Later, I understood that the aircraft had dropped many handbills and other papers that contained appeals to stop jute cultivation. There was neither radio nor television then, so this was a unique way of reaching the people directly. While directing that movie, I tried to link these two incidents.

Dipankar: *Matira Manisha* is entirely in Odia. Do you know Odia?

Mrinal-da: Not a word. Not when the offer came. But I had no option. My producer insisted that I had to make a film on Kalindi Charan Panigrahi's award-winning novel,

Matira Manisha. Kalindi babu was a highly respected intellectual of Odisha. His daughter Nandini Satpathy later became the chief minister of Odisha.

Dipankar: She was also a Union minister. So, was your producer an Odia?

Mrinal-da: No, he was a Gujarati, who had spent many years in Odisha. I told him frankly that I was not well-known for delivering hits and the market for Odia films was very small. So, the film might not be able to return the investment. But he replied that he would not mind as long as the film was made according to his taste. So, I could not back out. I had to spend about a month at a remote village in Odisha to work out the script. While I stayed there to understand how the story should be adapted for the language of film, I became acquainted with the music and sweetness of the Odia language. It is a pity that although we are keen to learn foreign languages, we do not bother with other Indian languages.

Dipankar: Mrinal-da, my question was about the autobiographical elements in the film.

Mrinal-da: I am coming to it. The story is set in a rural backdrop, everything happens in the village. But my hero is different, he wants to leave the village. He walks beside the railway tracks to watch trains passing by, he makes faces at the people sitting inside. His family is worried about him; he is not interested in anything, especially working in the fields. Meanwhile, his father passes away, his elder brother becomes the head of the family and the equations change.

Dipankar: But where is the Garuda?

Mrinal-da: Have patience, it is coming. One morning, with an ear-splitting sound, a plane suddenly appears in the sky, just like it appeared in the sky of Faridpur many, many years ago. The entire village rushes to the river to have a better look. My hero climbs a tree, tears a handful of leaves and tries to hurl them at the aircraft. That night he dreams of Garuda. The big bird carries the boy on his back for a long flight. Then there is a big bang, and everything becomes dark. The dream ends. My hero gets up, wakes his newly-wed wife and narrates the dream—everything. He speaks to her about the many wonders of Calcutta—the Howrah Bridge, national museum, the Kali temple. That was how I integrated my childhood memory with the storyline.

Dipankar: The airplane has featured in your cinema as a motif more than once.

Mrinal-da: Do you think so?

Dipankar: For example, we find planes in *Baishey Shravana*. You have just narrated the story of the airplane in *Matira Manisha*. Then, *Ek Din Pratidin* ends with a plane flying.

Mrinal-da: For that matter, *Matira Manisha* also ends with planes. When the boy finally leaves the village, aircrafts come and cover the sky. Do you recall that?

Dipankar: Yes. But here, what does the plane stand for?

Mrinal-da: Well, it can be a symbol of science and technology. I think to some extent, the relationship between the brothers also depended on science and its development. In addition to the films you mentioned, an aircraft plays a significant role in *Genesis* too. You can convey many things through a plane. As you look up at the sky, you can see so many things that earlier escaped you. I find it very important.

Dipankar: I feel I should point out that some other objects too have appeared in your films regularly. One such object is an old palatial building, dilapidated and semi-abandoned. A number of your films feature such buildings.

Mrinal-da: Yes, you are right. I would rather call them 'ruins', because that has a symbolic significance. Sometimes these buildings stand for society, sometimes for the relationship between two individuals. This happens not only in cinema but in other art forms also. Let me give you an example. Are you familiar with the works of Gabriel Garcia Marquez?

Dipankar: Of course. He is a master of modern fiction.

Mrinal-da: He is an old friend of mine; I knew him long before he received the Nobel Prize in literature. He is also closely associated with cinema. In fact, he headed the film school in Havana; I have been there too. One day, I was talking to him about his book, *The Autumn of the Patriarch*.

He told me, 'Mrinal, why don't you make a film on this book? I feel the subject is very Indian.'

I said, 'Is it so? I find it very Latin American. Why do you say it is Indian?'

Then Marquez told me how he came to write that novel. He said that many years ago, he was going through a pictorial album of Indian architecture. There he found a photograph of an abandoned Indian palace, and as he looked at the photograph, he felt that it was a mine of stories—unknown tales were hidden in that abandoned palace. That was how the idea of the book was born.

Dipankar: Do you also see stories in the ruins?

Mrinal-da: I feel my films grow with the ruins. This happened with *Baishey Shravana* and many other films. Marquez—I used to call him Gabba—once asked me how my ideas bloomed. I told him that it was a very internal process, I would not be able to describe or explain it. Gabba told me about his method. He would think about a visual image, like the photo of the abandoned palace, and then his imagination would take over. I said, 'You are a writer, so that works fine with you. But my method is different.'

Dipankar: What exactly is your method?

Mrinal-da: I love mountains, oceans, human beings, their faces and expressions—and I love those ruins just as much. That is why they come back in my films again and again.

Dipankar: Even in your last film, *Antareen*, this idea of a ruin—

Mrinal-da: I beg your pardon. *Antareen* is not my last film. It is only my most recent work. I am not going to die before making at least a couple of films of my choice.

Dipankar: That is good news for all of us.

Mrinal-da: Talking about *Antareen*, there are only two main characters in the movie. The boy lives in an old mansion, which is, of course, in ruins, but so is the nicely decorated affluent flat where the girl stays. The concept of a ruin works at different levels. Look at *Khandhar*. There is an old bedridden woman, who can neither see nor move. Even her abode is literally falling apart. I think both the lady and where she lives should be called ruins.

Dipankar: So, now we know that aircrafts and old mansions attract and excite you. In your life, have these two ever met?

Mrinal-da: Let me make one thing clear. I am not an archaeologist, I live only for the present. I only try to link the past with the present. I have never treated the relics of the past as museum pieces but rather made them part of life.

Dipankar: This is rather confusing.

Mrinal-da: I can try to clarify by narrating an incident. But this will be longish.

Dipankar: Please go ahead. This is the Mrinal-da I am trying to understand…

Mrinal-da: Not very long ago, I was in Rome, going around the ancient buildings. Shabana Azmi, the noted actress, was also with me. One afternoon, we stood before the Colosseum, the legendary palace of Emperor Nero. For quite some time, we just stood speechless. After a while, Shabana came out of her trance, whispered 'Fantastic!' and started moving around. A number of noticeboards have been put up there. She took out a notebook and wrote down the contents of those boards. I just walked from one ruin to another. Then I heard a sound and looked up: two helicopters were floating just above the ancient monument.

On our way back, Shabana playfully asked me, 'Mrinal-da, could you hear Nero playing his fiddle?'

I replied, 'No, all I heard was the noise of the helicopters, but no icon of Christ was hanging from those flying machines.'

Shabana immediately responded, 'But there was neither Marcello nor the paparazzi.'

The exchange of words with Shabana was quite amusing. I kept thinking, how easily we have entered the world of *La Dolce Vita*. Shabana suddenly became serious and uttered, 'What a contrast!'

A helicopter flying atop the Colosseum had made her think of Nero's fiddle. I told her, 'But I think this is coexistence. Both are an integral part of our life.'

I do not know whether Shabana accepted my theory, but I firmly believe that the past and present do get intertwined in our life.

Dipankar: I have not heard this story before. But you often narrate a similar account, your experience at Dhauli in Odisha.

Mrinal-da: But long before that something eerie happened to me, which I can now tell you about. On the face of it, it is very ordinary, but deep down, it may not be that easy to explain. Anyway, let me try.

Dipankar: Please go ahead.

Mrinal-da: I visited Sarnath for the first time in January 1952. I had nothing to do with films then, I was a mere peddler of medicines, or in polite language, a medical representative. After looking at the Ashoka Chakra and other monuments, I noticed some rooms down a staircase.

The guide told me that the monks in ancient times lived in and used those rooms. Out of curiosity I went down and stood before a room. There was no proper door, just a frame-like opening to enter through. When I tried to enter, I found that I was taller than the frame, so I had to bow to enter the room. The moment I bent over to enter the room, something happened inside me, and I felt I was a monk living in that room. How that happened, I do not know. But once I came out and stood straight, I once again became my normal self, a medicine peddler.

Dipankar: Have you found an explanation?

Mrinal-da: All I can say is that a Buddhist monk has to bow many times during a day. This is something that is part of his meditation, his worship and his rituals. As I bowed to enter the room, something snapped, and the door between the past and the present somehow opened. I feel that through these two insignificant events in my life, there was an attempt to link the past and the present.

Dipankar: Would you place the Dhauli incident in the same category?

Mrinal-da: Let me explain to you what happened at Dhauli. Dhauli was the capital of the ancient Kalinga, that is, present-day Odisha. There was a massive battle between the armies of Emperor Ashoka and the local king. It was a real do-or-die battle; legend says the nearby Daya River had no water, only blood flowed there. On a hot summer afternoon, I landed there to select a location for my documentary on Indian history. Dhauli also has some rock edicts of Ashoka, which I wanted to see.

Dipankar: Do you remember the year?

Mrinal-da: It was 1966. I was looking at the edicts when I felt that somebody was standing behind me. I saw a very old woman bent with age, a rickety stick in hand and a few goats grazing around her. I smiled and she smiled back. It was a toothless grin, but it led to instant magic; like Sarnath, somewhere a door had opened, and I walked through it to a distant past.

Dipankar: What did you see or feel this time?

Mrinal-da: I felt she was a witness to that massacre. Her entire family was butchered, her daughter raped, grandchildren thrown into a raging fire. The shell-shocked woman was still silently sitting there, where the edict even today proudly proclaims, 'I, dear to the Gods, Priyadarshi, I consider my subjects as my children…' Can you imagine how cruel this declaration is to that woman?

Dipankar: I think this springs from your perception of history. The historian Toynbee probably had a vision of King Darius leading an expedition to Greece while visiting one of those ancient Greek sites. It seems you were not particularly fond of Emperor Ashoka.

Mrinal-da: Let me tell you something interesting. Ashoka's edicts are scattered all over the country, and those edicts highlight how the Kalinga war transformed him, but the edicts at Dhauli are silent about it. Perhaps because the people of Kalinga never forgot his cruelty. I have no idea how he was as a person, but he was certainly a very cunning and diplomatic monarch.

Dipankar: Well, every successful monarch is. What about Akbar?

Mrinal-da: In this context, I can relate another historic event. The uprising of 1857, whether you call it a Sepoy Mutiny or the First War of Independence, was witness to unprecedented cruelty and savagery by the British. Hundreds of Indians were killed. In the following year, the British government took over the administration of India. Then came the proclamation by the queen. What was that proclamation? 'I, Victoria, the Queen of England and the Empress of India, my subjects…' etc., etc. The same lingo, the same format. Only the great queen was not required to place edicts all over the country, she had much better vehicles of communication at her command.

Dipankar: You mean that the intentions of the two monarchs are basically the same, only a few thousand years separate the two.

Mrinal-da: These have been my thoughts for many years, and it is possible to make a film on the subject. But I am not a historian in any sense of the term, and when I discussed my ideas with some professional historians, they did not show much excitement. Maybe there is something wrong with my thought process.

Dipankar: We have digressed far from cinema, but I think this detour was necessary to understand the inner you. Now, we should get back to your films.

Film After Film

Dipankar: Keeping in mind your aversion and allergy to your debut film, I have not even mentioned its name so far. But for the sake of history, let me put on record that your first film was *Raat Bhore*. Let us talk a little about it. Briefly, looking back, what do you think went wrong with *Raat Bhore*?

Mrinal-da: First of all, my knowledge of cinema at that time was basically academic. I had no concept of its technical aspect. The story was also highly melodramatic. I cannot say that the story was imposed on me. I knew it was not strong but felt that something interesting could be made out of it. So, I am the villain of the piece, handicapped by the choice of a weak story and lack of technical knowledge. Very briefly, I failed to deliver. Neither aesthetically nor in terms of style, could I deliver. Please do not ask me anything more. Even now, I hate the film so much that I do not even utter its name. I was so devastated by it that I even thought about giving up cinema for good.

Dipankar: We are lucky that you changed your mind.

Mrinal-da: My next film was based on some personal experiences of the noted Hindi poet Mahadevi Varma. The story was based on her interactions with a Chinese salesman. In the 1930s, lots of smooth-talking Chinese salesmen and hawkers could be seen around Calcutta's New Market area. I was initially appointed to write the script only, but subsequently the producer asked me to direct the film as well. My producer was the well-known singer-composer Hemanta Mukhopadhyay; the film was called *Neel Akasher Neechey.*

Dipankar: I think this was Hemanta babu's first film as a producer.

Mrinal-da: Yes. The story revolves around two characters—the heroine of the film who is a die-hard Congress worker and wears only khadi, and the hero who is a Chinese salesman who wants to palm off some Chinese silk and such stuff to her, but she firmly refuses and says, 'Look, I do not use foreign stuff.'

This chap retorts, 'But I am not a foreigner. My eyes are not blue, I have a flat nose—how can I be a foreigner?'

The idea being that only people from imperialist countries are foreigners, the rest are not.

Dipankar: Wasn't the storyline a bit sentimental?

Mrinal-da: I agree. In fact, everything about the film is very sentimental, and now when I talk about it, I am somewhat embarrassed by it as well. Structurally also, it has many weak spots. But I still stand by its political viewpoint.

Dipankar: What was that?

Mrinal-da: I tried to convey that our freedom struggle was in tune with the struggles in other countries fighting for democracy. In fact, fights against imperialism and fascism are identical. I still feel that I was right in my thinking. That is why our first prime minister, Jawaharlal Nehru, liked it so much. I can't say it is my favourite movie, but from there, I started moving in right direction.

Dipankar: Your next movie was *Baishey Shravana*. We have already discussed how you looked at the Great Bengal Famine, so let us look at it from a different angle. Mrinal-da, in this film, you have taken the camera out of the studio for a long stretch. It was your first truly outdoor shoot, or, to use film lingo, it was primarily based on location shooting. In later years too, location shooting plays an important role in your cinema. Would you like to comment on this?

Mrinal-da: I did not find the concept of location shooting to be very novel, because as I told you before, *Chinnamul* by Nemai Ghosh was shot entirely on location. While I understood its importance in documentary films, for popular cinema I did not understand its importance till I saw *Pather Panchali*. That film, except the night sequences, was shot entirely on location. It was only after watching *Pather Panchali* that I seriously thought about location shooting and tried to develop my scripts keeping in mind the importance of location. That is what you get to see in *Baishey Shravana*. I do not hesitate to admit that my thinking about film-making was seriously influenced by Satyajit Ray, whom I used to call Manik babu. But stylistically, I have a major difference with Manik babu. I have heard that before shooting, he always wrote a complete script and followed it strictly.

Dipankar: This is my impression too. But I wanted to know whether location shooting had an impact on your style as a film-maker.

Mrinal-da: Look, I have regularly shot both inside and outside the studio. For example, *Bhuvan Shome* was almost entirely shot outside, on location. But I never had a watertight script like Manik babu. Location has played an interesting role in my narrative; occasionally location has also changed the storyline. Many of my location shooting sequences that have been widely appreciated were not there in the original script. After taking a shot at a location, I start thinking about what the next shot should be; because in a location shooting, characters before the camera often react in a way that I did not anticipate, so how can I write it down in advance? So, as you shoot, you keep reworking your script.

Dipankar: I have read that Fellini followed the same method of improvisation.

Mrinal-da: (*Laughs*) But he never admitted it. In the United States, he was once asked—'Why do you improvise so much?' He denied it angrily, stating that film-making was like mathematics, with every step precalculated. Liberties like improvisation couldn't be taken. Then he added that he kept his eyes and ears open, so if anything occurred around him, it would find a place in his movie.

Dipankar: Do you follow the same path?

Mrinal-da: I openly admit that I improvise; I also enjoy improvising. In fact, that is what I have been telling you all along. But I must also say that one aspect of film-making that I consider most important is editing, and I have mastered it. My films are made on the editing table by arranging shots. In this process, the film is often quite different from the original script; even my thinking during the shooting is not always reflected in the final version.

Dipankar: We will come back to editing later. Since we are talking about location, we can take another jump cut and from *Baishey Shravana* go to *Akaler Sandhane*, twenty years later. The two films had some similarities, and I have heard that you had thought about shooting both films at the same location.

Mrinal-da: Yes, you are right. But two decades is a pretty long period. In *Baishey Shravana*, you will hear references to the Great War and the Bengal famine, but it is neither a war film nor a famine movie. Famine was the backdrop; the story is centred on a man-woman relationship, in this case between a pretty girl and her not particularly good-looking husband, but some foreigners found him manly and attractive.

Dipankar: Was famine only a backdrop in *Baishey Shravana?*

Mrinal-da: Well, it was something more than that. I think famine was the catalyst. How the relationship between a husband and his wife is corroded, how men slowly lose their moral bearing. This film depicts those intricacies of the relationship in the physical presence of famine. Without the famine, the erosion of the relationship would not have happened. Am I clear?

Dipankar: To some extent, yes.

Mrinal-da: But *Akaler Sandhane* is a different ball game. In 1980, a film unit from Calcutta invades a remote, godforsaken village in Bengal to shoot a film on the Bengal famine. There is a continuous interaction between the past and the present there. The past regularly gatecrashes the present because my thesis is the famine is a continuous process. Not just with regard to food, but in many more things in life it is very much on. So, the film has many layers.

Dipankar: There is also a film-within-a-film in *Akaler Sandhane.*

Mrinal-da: It does have many layers. One of them is the relationship between a dying old man and his wife. My wife plays that role in the film. It is extremely difficult to direct one's wife because the director's impartiality can be questioned. She had no role in *Baishey Shravana*, but here she is the wife of the old landlord. I am not sure whether he should be called a landlord, because there is very little land left. All he has is a huge palace-like building … that also dilapidated.

Dipankar: So, one more ruin.

Mrinal-da: Right, one more ruin. I shot the film at a place called Somrabazar, a small village, barely two and a half hours' drive from Calcutta. *Baishey Shravana* was shot at Mankar in Bardhaman district. After twenty years, I returned there to explore the possibility of making *Akaler Sandhane* there. It was a strange journey, almost like a pilgrimage.

A boy of about twenty came up to me and touched my feet. He said, 'You won't know me, sir, but I was born during the shooting of your film.'

Immediately I remembered the incident and recalled, 'That morning, your father was very anxious and restless, because your mother was already in labour, and the nearest hospital was eight miles away. So, one of the unit cars took her to the hospital for delivery. So, you are that boy?'

It would have been great fun if we could have shot there.

Dipankar: Fun in what sense?

Mrinal-da: Away from the script. Just imagine a villager approaches the director and says, 'Oh, you have come to shoot a film. Twenty years ago, a tall, dark, lean and undernourished fellow had also come to shoot a film, I think it was called *Baishey Shravana.* I think his name was, er, Mrinal Sen. Do you know where that bloke is now?' Wouldn't that be funny?

Dipankar: Yes, definitely. You could have added another layer to the film. But then, why did you choose another location?

Mrinal-da: The house in Mankar was in such pathetic condition that I felt scared. It was too risky. But during the shooting, I was overwhelmed by *Baishey Shravana.* While on location for *Akaler Sandhane* I had written a letter to Gita, my wife, which I found a few days ago while rummaging through some old papers. The letter refreshed my memory, and I remembered some interesting seminaries.

Dipankar: Please tell us.

Mrinal-da: The letter is dated 24 September 1980. Gita had finished her shooting and had returned to Calcutta. I wrote that the previous night I had had a strange dream. In the dream I had found myself at the Mankar building. I told you that the lord of the house was bedridden and paralysed and he could hardly speak. But in my dream, he was standing erect, and asked me in a rich baritone, 'Who are you, my son?'

Dipankar: But, you did show the old man's death in *Akaler Sandhane*.

Mrinal-da: Believe me that was not in the original script. I got up in the morning, still a bit disturbed by the dream. I immediately inserted a new sequence—the old man had died in his sleep. All the village veterans had assembled in the mansion. My heroine, Smita (Patil), had spent the whole night with the landlord's wife. Smita came out of the room in the morning and told the production controller that a unit car had to go to a nearby village to fetch the only daughter of the aged couple. Only then could the cremation be arranged. The director said that should not be a problem. After breakfast, I wrote the sequence, had a couple of quick rehearsals and shot it. If I had not had that dream, this sequence would not have been there.

Dipankar: This sequence is similar to the incident that you mentioned occurred when shooting *Baishey Shravana.* I am referring to sending the pregnant lady to hospital in a unit car.

Mrinal-da: Exactly. I just fine-tuned that incident and put it there. Such funny things do happen on location.

Dipankar: I am going back to *Raat Bhore* for a second. You had said that you had no idea about the technical aspect of movie-making. When did you grasp it?

Mrinal-da: Right from *Baishey Shravana*, I started working on that aspect. But there is something I want to clarify. Some film critics have discovered similarities between *Pather Panchali* and *Baishey Shravana*, which I do not find. The fact that both films are based on the lives of rural, low-income-group people or that in both films two old ladies die are not important resemblances—at least according to me.

Dipankar: May I add that both deaths signify the end of an era.

Mrinal-da: Okay, I accept that. Yet I would emphasize that there is a fundamental difference between the two films. In my film, there are excellent shots showing nature in its various aspects, but you won't find a single shot where there is no human face. I am never attracted by nature's beauty if it has no relationship to our daily life. But I must admit and put on record that *Pather Panchali* encouraged and helped me to move forward. That included technical excellence.

Dipankar: But, I think your most notable film, technically, is *Akash Kusum*. Would you agree?

Mrinal-da: Undoubtedly. In that film, I literally played with the camera and other equipment, like a child plays with his blocks and other toys.

Dipankar: Were you influenced by any film-maker?

Mrinal-da: It is no secret that around that time, I had watched some films made by Truffaut, and those films influenced me profoundly. So, in 1965, when I directed *Akash Kusum,* I used cartloads of freeze shots. Now, I feel that I overdid it a bit. But you must remember that times were changing. I felt that as a film-maker of a new school of thought, I must set up a new frontier that was different from my predecessors. If some excesses happened in the process, so be it.

Dipankar: *Akash Kusum* marks the end of the first decade of your film career. If we look back, we find that you worked largely with established actors and technicians of Tollygunge, there was not much experimentation or breaking new ground. Would you agree?

Mrinal-da: Not entirely. Look at *Baishey Shravana.* Madhabi (Mukhopadhyay) was virtually a new face, it was only her second film. Jnanesh (Mukherjee) was a seasoned actor, but he was essentially a stage artiste. As husband and wife they looked so different, so poles apart that people used to tell my producer, 'They are the oddest couple of Bengali cinema; why are you wasting your hard-earned money on them?'

Dipankar: Around that period, you also tried your hand at making comedies. But I feel you never liked them.

Mrinal-da: Right you are. But to be honest, even now I am not fully happy with any of my films. Since invariably I happen to be my first audience, I have always felt that had this been a rehearsal, I would have made so many changes. When people admire my work, I am naturally happy, but at the back of my mind, I am also a bit uncomfortable, because nobody knows the shortcomings more than I do. I am sure I am not the only one with such feelings, other creative persons must feel the same.

Dipankar: Don't tell me you are not fully satisfied with any of your film?

Mrinal-da: (*With a smile*) Do you know what I do whenever I compose a good sequence or take a good shot? I run to the washroom, because there, I am all alone. I stand before the mirror and tell myself—'Mrinal Sen, you are a genius, otherwise how could you have done it?' This is how I am happy or unhappy. If you ask me to remake all my films, I probably won't be able to do that. If I have a longer life, I may try.

Dipankar: Have you ever thought, like Hitchcock or Mehboob Khan, to remake one of your own films?

Mrinal-da: Yes, I have thought many times about making a film afresh, just as I sometimes wish to restart my life. Mind you, I have lived a long and fulfilling life, I have nothing to complain about. Still, I long to live my life afresh. Like the protagonist of my film *Ek Din Achanak*. If I could start life again, I would probably take totally different decisions.

Dipankar: Let us go back to *Akash Kusum*. There is a feeling that the film never got its due. It is a fascinating analysis of the hopes, aspirations and failures of the middle class, the Bengali bhadralok. In my opinion, from the points of view of technique and content, the film was made much before its time, so the general audience failed to appreciate it. The film was also involved in some avoidable and unnecessary controversy. I am referring to the long-drawn bitter epistolary war fought in the columns of *The Statesman*.

Mrinal-da: (*Laughs*) Even a person of the stature of Satyajit Ray played a major role in it.

Dipankar: At this juncture, would you like to make an assessment of two of your eminent contemporaries? I am referring to Ray and Ritwik Ghatak.

Mrinal-da: (*After a pause*) It is probably better not to raise the issue here. They were both extremely powerful film-makers, and I can say a lot about them, because all of us worked at the same time and we all have our angularities. With full respect to them I can only say that sometimes I felt uncomfortable and even disappointed with their work. I need not say anything more.

Dipankar: Is that all?

Mrinal-da: Yes, that is all.

Dipankar: Well, if you feel so, I must respect your wishes. *Akash Kusum* was followed by *Matira Manisha*, a low-budget Odia movie that did not run well, but it occupies an important place in your filmography because of its autobiographical element, which we have already discussed. In this film, your concept about the interrelationship between cinema and literature took definite shape. Let us delve a little deeper into that aspect of cinema.

Cinema and Literature

Dipankar: Mrinal-da, most of your movies are based on published literary works. How do you see the interrelationship between these two mediums of art?

Mrinal-da: I feel there is a continuous reaction between the two, in fact, there is constant turmoil. Earlier, a film was just a chain of events; now the emphasis is on feelings. Look at Tagore's *Ghare Baire*. It is a conventional story, narrated by three different persons. But due to Tagore's genius, one character does not start at the same point where the other has left off. The story sometimes moves forward, sometimes backward. I think while making the film on the story, Ray had said in an interview that he would try to incorporate a fourth point of view, that of the film-maker. Had he been able to do it, it would have become something brilliant. Unfortunately, the final product became just a conventional love triangle.

The French Nouvelle Vague of the fifties that shook up the film world was influenced by modern French novels, but British and American film-makers were not impressed by the novels of Virginia Woolf and James Joyce. Eisenstein was furious when the Soviet Union banned *Ulysses*. He said that Russian readers would be deprived of a great treasure. You probably know that before writing the script of *An American Tragedy*, he went to Paris to meet James Joyce and had a long discussion on how to use internal monologue in cinema.

Dipankar: But would you call *An American Tragedy* unconventional?

Mrinal-da: There is an anomaly. Eisenstein wanted to end the film on the protagonist's hesitation about murdering the girl, but the producer insisted on a crime thriller.

Dipankar: Do you think that cinema can become independent of literature?

Mrinal-da: Why? This dependence has continued for so many years, enriching both art forms. Why should you break it? Why would I not pick up from other art forms like music and visual art? While making *Oka Oori Katha*, I listened to Burrakatha in Andhra Pradesh. Have you heard about it? It is a unique art form.

Dipankar: No. What is it?

Mrinal-da: Suppose someone is telling you stories from the Mahabharata. Suddenly he brings in a current happening, some local issue, then goes back to the Mahabharata. I found this form very cinematic. Have you read Banaphool's *Mrigayaa*? It is part drama, part poetry, as if the author is playing with multiple formats. This is how walls are broken constantly between various art forms.

Dipankar: Mrinal-da, as a film-maker, what do you look for when you read a story?

Mrinal-da: This is very difficult to answer. This is what Mao Zedong calls a Surprise Attack.

Dipankar: At least tell me—is cinema an extension of literature or a recreation of literature?

Mrinal-da: I think it is both. Both these art forms meet at a certain point. J.B. Priestly wrote some time plays, where the story just ends at a given point. What I think of a story in the morning may not be what I think of it in the evening because I have been enriched by a whole day's experiences. This is recreation, and it is a continuous process.

Dipankar: But in such cases, the film may move away from the original story, as it often happens with your cinema.

Mrinal-da: Yes, it does. There is hardly any similarity between *Abirata Chenamukh* and *Ek Din Pratidin*. Yet, the literary text helps me, rather it provokes me to make the film. You can say it is my starting point. Sometimes, nothing more.

Dipankar: Then I would ask, why do you go to an author, if you are not faithful to his text?

Mrinal-da: Because there is no alternative. This is when you try to extend and recreate something. I need an alternative view of society, of people, emotions, and a story gives me that.

Dipankar: But are you being fair, morally and ethically?

Mrinal-da: The moment I begin to read a story, the journey of cinema begins. When the film ends, it may not have anything to do with the original story. That is why I scrupulously avoid Bengali classics, I mean the works of Bankim Chandra, Tagore and Sarat Chandra, because my end point may not tally with the main text. I feel while making a film, you have to satisfy three mistresses. The first mistress is the text, which is the basis of my film; the second mistress is my medium, cinema. Cinema has its own language, own diction. I have to build up the story through that language, which has, apart from words, i.e., dialogue, two additional tools—visuals and sound. Then comes the third mistress and she is the most difficult one to please. I call her time or contemporaneity. That means the film must reflect the time I am living in. It is a difficult job, but film-making has never been easy.

Dipankar: You mean that the film-maker need not be faithful to the story?

Mrinal-da: If the text is so sacred, put it in a museum. As a film-maker, my job is to infuse contemporary feelings in my work, and for that I am ready to ignore the text, if need be.

Dipankar: This line of logic may be acceptable when you work with *Matira Manisha* or *Telenapota Abishkar*, because those stories were written in the 1930s, and some changes had to be incorporated. But let us take *Kharij*, which deals with contemporary reality. But here too you deviated from the storyline.

Mrinal-da: Well, you have chosen a fine example; let me elaborate. First of all, *Kharij* is not a film on child labour. My aim was to have a showdown with the middle class. The middle class is not bad, per se, but it has certain shortcomings. These people suffer from a tremendous guilt complex, and I basically played with that. While making the film, I realized that the story had certain problems, so I could not follow it blindly.

Dipankar: What problems?

Mrinal-da: Mostly related to details. The book gives the impression that asphyxia and carbon monoxide poisoning are the same thing. But they are two different things with different symptoms. I met the superintendent of Calcutta Medical College, had a long discussion with him and only then understood the issue and realized that these were all jumbled up in the book.

In this context, I put the man-woman relationship under the scanner. They started blaming each other. The husband tried to hide something from the police, which the wife blurted out. Their relationship took a nosedive when the child's father arrived. I had created the background at the very beginning through their conversation—she wanted this, she wanted that and ended the wishlist with a boy-servant, who would eat little and demand a low salary. Mind you, the conversation took place in the darkness of a moving cab, so we never see their faces. This was the beginning of the film, and at the end, the dead boy's father comes, performs the last rites of his son and leaves with a polite 'good night, sir'. This was like a big slap on everybody's face—an exposure of the dual value system of the middle class and the helplessness of the working class.

Dipankar: But did the author, Ramapada Chowdhury, appreciate the changes?

Mrinal-da: Oh yes! After the premiere, he almost danced with joy, 'What a fabulous movie!' But nothing that I told you was in his text. In the book, there is a Naxalite boy, a court scene, the protagonist's affair with a junior lady lawyer—to me all that was irrelevant stuff.

Dipankar: How have the other literary luminaries whose works you have used reacted to your treatment of their works?

Mrinal-da: When I approached Premendra Mitra for the rights to his story *Telenapota Abishkar*, he had just one condition—'Mrinal, you must complete the film before I go blind.' His eyes were in a very bad state at that time.

Dipankar: He did go completely blind in his last days.

Mrinal-da: Fortunately, I was able to show him *Khandhar*, and he liked it. After the screening, I told him, 'Premendra, I had to change your story drastically.'

He replied, 'It does not matter. You have retained the spirit.'

Banaphool, author of *Bhuvan Shome*, was not that happy, but he accepted the changes sportingly. His beautiful comment after the screening was, 'Actually, this is Mrinal Sen's *Bhuvan Shome*, but it is partially mine.'

Dipankar: You went back to Ramapada babu again, for *Ek Din Achanak.*

Mrinal-da: Again, details became an issue. I asked him, 'How did the professor draw his pension? By cheque or by cash?' He looked at me blankly and replied, 'I have no clue.' Again, I had to call on a bank manager to understand the system.

Dipankar: We started our conversation on literature and cinema with *Matira Manisha.* I want to go back to it again. There was a controversy regarding the film—will you put on record what the controversy was?

Mrinal-da: As I have already told you, the film was based on a novel of the same name. The literary work was specially acclaimed in Odisha. Kalindi Charan Panigrahi wrote it in the 1930s; I was shooting it in 1965-66. In those three decades, society had changed tremendously, and I wanted to integrate the changes in the film. The book was based on a joint family of two brothers. I got the impression from the book that Kalindi babu obliquely blamed the wife of the younger brother for the split in the family. I did not support the allegation. See, the elder brother got married when both parents were alive, and they controlled the household. After the parents died, the mantle passed to the elder brother and his wife, which was resented by the younger brother's wife, who thought they were equals, and so she too should get the same privileges. This does not mean that she wanted to split the family. In the film, I gave her my full support. This was not appreciated by the Odia academics.

Dipankar: To think differently from the author's point of view seems to be a favourite tendency.

Mrinal-da: Maybe. To me a story is my take-off point. In recent times, after I made *Antareen*, a lover of Urdu literature asked me the name of the story I had used for the film. It seemed he went through the complete works of Manto but could not identify the story. I recollected that even Amrit Rai, son of Munshi Premchand, could not find his father's story in my film *Oka Oori Katha*.

Dipankar: Does this appear rather strange even to you?

Mrinal-da: I love it! In 1978, I made the film *Oka Oori Katha* in Telugu based on Premchand's last short story, *Kafan*. Let me clarify that I do not know even one word of Telugu. After the film was ready, I invited Amrit Rai for the screening. You may be aware that he was also an Akademi award-winning writer and his father's biographer.

After the screening, he embraced me and said, 'Mrinal, it was a shattering experience, but I do not agree with your interpretation of the story.'

I told him, 'Your father would probably have said the same. But tell me, are you unhappy that you gave me the film rights?'

He replied, 'By no means. It is a brilliant film. In future also, you can make a film on any of my father's stories; I am giving you permission in advance. Yet, I must place on record that I do not accept your interpretation.'

Dipankar: Do you accept that if you change the basic structure of a story, the author feels hurt?

Mrinal-da: My attitude is as I have said before—literature is a reflection of society, it cannot be, I insist that it is not, a museum piece; it must be relevant to contemporary society. This is true of all literary works. Look at Michael Madhusudan. He was a rebel, whose rebellion was against the orthodoxy of nineteenth-century Hindu society. He wrote an epic based on the Ramayana but dared to comment, 'I hate Rama and his rabble. My sympathy is with Ravana.' Don't you think Madhusudan's rebellion has enriched our culture, our literary heritage?

Dipankar: Undoubtedly.

Mrinal-da: Then look at Irawati Karve, a Maharashtrian academic who looked at the Mahabharata from a refreshingly new angle. I am not a literary expert, so I should not say more. The Mahabharata is an ancient literary text, which Karve reinterpreted. If this is possible in literature, why not in cinema?

Dipankar: Are you inspired by modern Bengali literature?

Mrinal-da: Honestly speaking, I find the language very facile and easy-flowing, but nothing more. I go through the stories and then try to get something out of them. This is possible only in the works of Ramapada Chowdhury. He provides a new level, sort of an undercurrent, beneath the stories. Tagore is at the other extreme; he describes everything and leaves nothing for the reader's imagination. I find it very frustrating if I cannot participate in the creative process. Personally, I like the works of Kamal Kumar Majumdar, but I feel the architecture of his language just cannot be translated into cinema; cinema has a different grammar. Same is the problem with my friend, Gabba, better known as Gabriel Garcia. Not a single good film has come out of his fiction.

Dipankar: Are you suggesting that good cinema cannot come out of experimental writing?

Mrinal-da: Not necessarily, because experiments can be of many types. I believe an outstanding film can come out of Tagore's *Chhinnapatra.* While talking about *Kharij*, I missed an important point. May I add that?

Dipankar: Yes, of course.

Mrinal-da: Do you remember the character of Hari in the film?

Dipankar: (*After a pause*) Yes, I do. Hari was the landlord's boy-servant.

Mrinal-da: In the entire film, Hari does not utter a single word, he just watches, moving around uselessly. The elders do not like it at all, but they cannot do anything about it.

Dipankar: Would you call him the conscience of the master-class?

Mrinal-da: I think much more than that. His face and movements reflect the exploitation. At the post-screening press conference at the Cannes Film Festival, a foreigner had commented, 'In this boy's face, I can see the ruined economy of a village.' Strangely, nobody here observed it. It did not even strike the author. Sometimes, I also wonder how I conceived it.

Dipankar: In the 1930s, Tagore wrote a letter to one Murari Bhaduri, expressing his ideas about the interrelation between the two art forms. Would you like to comment on it?

Mrinal-da: I think it was an on-the-spur-of-the-moment reaction, and we need not take it too seriously. Because with all due respect, cinema was not his domain, he did not get the opportunity to watch many films. Cinema is an independent medium, but, as we have discussed, there is no partition wall between the two. I think there is a continuous process of cross-fertilization.

Dipankar: But does cinema have its own language?

Mrinal-da: In 1924, D.W. Griffith had remarked, 'I can feel that sound is coming, and it will increase the dimension of cinema.' This is the way the language of cinema has evolved. From the time of Creation, human beings have tried to communicate with each other. First probably there was mime, and then came language. Even before the written script evolved, humans told stories and listened to stories. So, it is possible to make films without literature.

Dipankar: How can that happen?

Mrinal-da: Before answering that question, we must define literature. Would you call *Das Kapital* literature? Or for that matter, *Manifesto of The Communist Party*? But Eisenstein thought of making a script out of it. Do you remember the Fernando Solanas movie, *The Hour of the Furnaces*? A heavy and didactic film, it is like an essay. In the closing sequence, there is a three-minute-long close-up of Che Guevara, and the audience is forced to have an eyeball-to-eyeball confrontation with Che. This is also cinema. You can do anything with your camera. I also once threatened to make a film based on the lead editorial of the *Economic Times*. You can make a film on anything—a good story, bad story, even no-story; it is the way you use the camera and your creativity. How it turns out is another matter.

Dipankar: I still cannot comprehend how you can make a film without literature or written text.

Mrinal-da: Just because you have pen and paper, you cannot create literature; similarly, just because you have eyes, you cannot see or make films. Films do not come out of reading, they can even come out of listening.

Dipankar: I find it difficult to agree…

Mrinal-da: Just after the Kargil war, I was watching a television programme. A smart, young journalist was walking along the roads of Islamabad, asking various questions to all and sundry. He encountered a pavement seller and asked him what the war had given him. The man faced the camera and uttered just a single word—'*Nuksan*' (Loss). In that one word, I could see so many things, not only loss of life and property, but also the sense of losing respect and even civilization. Maybe one day I will make a film based on this one word. I can.

Dipankar: We would all welcome that happy occasion. But before we reach the conclusion of this particular topic, I have one more question for you. You are probably the only film-maker who has made films in four languages—two of them totally unknown to you.

Mrinal-da: Is that so? Maybe.

Dipankar: Do you feel like undertaking any more such ventures? A film in a fifth language as well?

Mrinal-da: Yes, very recently, I seriously considered making a film in Malayalam.

Dipankar: Now, my query is, are you not seriously handicapped in making a film in a language you do not know? How can you be sure that whatever you want to communicate in the film is faithfully reflected in the script, especially in the dialogues?

Mrinal-da: You are absolutely right. But I took that problem as a challenge. There is nothing like making a film in your mother tongue. Since you have command over the language, you can turn, twist and split the dialogues to highlight your characters. I have made a number of films in Hindi, a language I understand, even claim to know, people liked them too, but every time I have felt, how nice it would have been to make them in Bengali! But as you get into the process of film-making in a different language, you begin to learn a little about the language, the society…

Dipankar: Have you learnt a bit of Hindi over the years?

Mrinal-da: That is what I asked Shabana a few days ago, because she has acted in a few of my Hindi movies. Her reply was quite interesting. She said, 'Your language has not actually improved, but you have become more desperate with Hindi.' Well, I can be desperate while talking, but not so while making a movie.

Dipankar: Do you have a special method for making a film in a different language?

Mrinal-da: I always write my script in Bengali. After the script is ready, I have a session with someone who knows Bengali as well as the other language. I tell him, 'This is my version. You please tell me your version in your language, but no literal translation please; I want to get the feel of your language.' The actors also help me a lot in this process. This is how I shot films in Hindi and Odia.

Dipankar: Mrinal-da, as a metropolitan Bengali, I am sure you can follow basic Hindi and some words of Odia. But Telugu is a different ball game. That is one language you do not know at all. How did you manage to make a film in Telugu?

Mrinal-da: My Telugu movie *Oka Oori Katha* was based on Munshi Premchand's *Kafan*, a Hindi story. The story is set in a village in Uttar Pradesh in winter. While writing the script, I had thought of a village in Bengal, but while shooting, the location was shifted to a village in Telangana. As you know, winter is severe in Uttar Pradesh, it is milder in Bengal, and there is hardly any winter in the Telangana region. The theme of the film was poverty and exploitation, so the weather did not really matter. But what mattered was the language.

Dipankar: Did your tried-and-tested method fail?

Mrinal-da: Yes, you may say so. While one person gave me a Telugu rendering of the script, another man read it and told me it was trash. I was at my wits' end.

Dipankar: Ultimately, what was the solution?

Mrinal-da: I had to approach P. Sundarayya. Have you heard the name of Comrade Sundarayya?

Dipankar: Of course. He was the general secretary of the CPI(M).

Mrinal-da: More importantly, he knew the Telangana region like the palm of his hand. When I asked him for help, he said, 'Don't worry. I will give you my hand-picked man, Krishnamurthy, who will stay with you throughout the shooting and help you in every possible way.' It was no exaggeration. This man Krishnamurthy became an inseparable part of my unit from day one.

Dipankar: One final query about the film. Why did you choose Mamata Shankar for the role of an Andhra girl?

Mrinal-da: Because there is a pan-Indian quality in the appearance of Mamata. Smita (Patil) too had that look. You could pass them off as South Indian, Marathi, Gujarati—anything. Thanks to Krishnamurthy's guidance and his grasp of the local language, the film came out with flying colours, and I also picked up some gems from the local language. Having made films in many languages, I still insist that the pleasure of making a film in your mother tongue is unique and you never get it by making a film in any other language.

The Indian New Wave Cinema

Dipankar: Mrinal-da, don't you find it strange that the one film that brought you instant fame and success, one of your most outstanding films, *Bhuvan Shome*, was made in Hindi?

Mrinal-da: Well, *Bhuvan Shome* was an exceptional film in all respects; it had many 'firsts' to its credit. You know, the film was financed by the Film Finance Corporation, which has since become the National Film Development Corporation or NFDC. The corporation's rule was that to get financing, the film-maker had to apply with a full script. A committee would go through it and only after its approval would other formalities start.

Dipankar: Yes, I know the rules.

Mrinal-da: But the fact is I never submitted a script.

Dipankar: How could that be!

Mrinal-da: My friend Arun Kaul locked me up in his office in Bombay, threatening that he wouldn't open the door till I finished the script. After five hours and probably five gallons of tea, all I was able to produce was an eight-page treatment. I had been pondering over *Bhuvan Shome* for some time, as I had bought the rights about ten years ago. I was sure that no private producer would invest in the project.

Arun read the eight-page treatment and told me, 'Mrinal-da, there is no chance of getting any money, I can try if you agree to make the film in Hindi.'

So, I said, 'Let it be in Hindi then.'

Do you know this was the first FFC film for which I did not give a bank guarantee or any other surety? And it was a film that had no star cast and was shorter than the stipulated length?

Dipankar: Sorry, I don't understand, how can you know the length before you shoot the film?

Mrinal-da: Even you do not know this. Well, then, be enlightened. After the loan was sanctioned, I got the contract—a thirty-six-page document. With great difficulty, I read the first three or four pages and realized that I would no doubt serve a term in jail as there were too many restrictions that I would definitely violate. So, I just signed on the last page and mailed it back. In due course, the money came, the princely amount of a lakh and fifty thousand rupees, the money was spent and the film was made and those who gave the money liked it too. But there was a hitch. Somewhere in that thirty-six-page document, there was a clause that the film's minimum length must be 13,000 feet, but my film was only 9,600 feet. The powers-that-be brought this to my notice. I replied, 'Sorry, I can't do anything now, you better delete that clause.' I think they took my advice.

Dipankar: Do you think that the film's language contributed to its success?

Mrinal-da: I think the film had a freshness that appealed to the audience. It was made during an exciting time. All of us wanted to do something new. Hindi was new to me, it was my protagonist Utpal's (Dutt) first Hindi film. My heroine, Suhasini, was totally fresh, she had not even acted on stage; it was the first feature film of my music director, Vijaya Raghav Rao, and it was the first time that a student of the Pune film institute handled a camera independently. His name was K.K. Mahajan.

Dipankar: It is generally believed that *Bhuvan Shome* was the pioneer of the Indian New Wave. What is your thought on this?

Mrinal-da: (*With a smile*) Well, it is nice to hear such pleasant things. But whether that is right or wrong, you people should decide. I cannot comment.

Dipankar: At least tell us what you tried to do through the film.

Mrinal-da: I feel that *Bhuvan Shome* changed the whole concept of film-making. No one had made a film before with such a low budget. This was very important for me, because I have always heard from the commercial film lobby that cinema is an expensive medium. I tried to prove that it was possible to make a good film without spending too much.

Dipankar: This I feel is the external aspect; I am interested in the philosophy of the movement.

Mrinal-da: My aim was to go beyond the boundary drawn by my seniors. I was also attracted to non-narrative cinema. Right from my college days, my favourite author was Aldous Huxley, whose writings contain very little 'story' element. But once I started making films, I of course made films based on narrative structure. Around 1963, the French New Wave films arrived in India. No doubt I was overwhelmed by them, but I never copied those films. That happened accidentally when the Moviola got stuck and I got the idea of a freeze shot in *Pratinidhi*. Lindsay Anderson has written that I got the concept of freeze frames from Truffaut's *The 400 Blows*, but I think I saw it first in a Billy Wilder movie.

Dipankar: But in *Akash Kusum* you were definitely influenced by *The 400 Blows*.

Mrinal-da: Yes, I have already told you about my use of freeze shots in the film. But I tried so many novelties there. I had no money to hire a rain machine. But there is a rainy-day sequence. So what could be the alternative? I went to the archives of the *Anandabazar Patrika* and *The Statesman*, got some stills of waterlogged streets and placed them on the screen with the sound of running water in the background. My audience was basically urban newspaper-readers; they immediately got the connection. There was a new dimension of reality.

Dipankar: Why did you choose *Bhuvan Shome*?

Mrinal-da: First of all, I already had the rights to the story and did not need to spend on the basic material. It was also written by an eminent Bengali writer, Balai Chand Mukhopadhyay, his pen name was Banaphool. I had read the story in 1958. A friend of mine, writer and poet Bimal Roy Chowdhury, thought it was great film material and pressed me to buy the film rights.

Finally, when I got the financing in 1968, I told the author, Banaphool, 'This delay is a blessing in disguise. In this decade I have seen and learnt a lot; now, I will make the film in a new way.'

He hesitantly asked, 'Will my story survive?'

I replied with lots of confidence, 'Definitely, but maybe in a new form.'

Dipankar: What sort of changes did you want to usher in through this film?

Mrinal-da: In our country, there was no New Wave or parallel cinema, because we were stuck in the physicality of cinema. Cinema has two basic components—camera and sound. But we could not go beyond these basics. Our cinema was focused on words and events. I started thinking, why can't we have more feelings and less events?

Dipankar: What strikes me most about the Indian New Wave is that in a particular period of time, talented filmmakers all over the country decided to make a particular type of cinema. How did that happen?

Mrinal-da: All of us were looking for something but did not know how to search, where to search. The one common point was that we all decided to be different from our seniors. My cinema is widely different from Mani Kaul's cinema. But there is one similarity, we followed no legacy, we did not inherit anything. This is true of everybody, be it Kumar (Shahani), Shyam (Benegal) or Adoor (Gopalakrishnan). This movement started in Calcutta; film societies helped trigger our imagination, and soon, like an epidemic, the lust for creating new cinema spread all over the country. It just happened, we did not plan it. In France, they all did it together, somebody wrote the script, another handled the camera, the third friend pushed the trolley. That was not possible here, but had it been so, the movement would have been stronger. Then there was that lurking fear that if two films flopped there was nothing but starvation ahead. That is why some people compromised, some even deserted. There is no halfway house, you prosper or perish.

Dipankar: I think the socio-economic situation of the seventies also contributed to its success.

Mrinal-da: In my case, it was my association with the IPTA. I have already told you about that and how that led to my entry into cinema. There was also a socio-political belief. But you are right, one's time, one's era, definitely influences one. I am the greatest example of this. I am doing nothing these days, the grey cells of my brain have probably turned white. But this peculiar vacuum around, the choking sterile emptiness around, believe me, I have never encountered this before. All I hear is empty words, in political speeches, in literature, in every sphere. And I don't feel like creating anything out of this hollowness.

Dipankar: If a person like you, with so much determination and talent, sits back quietly, what is the future of our New Wave cinema?

Mrinal-da: That I cannot tell you, I am not a soothsayer. I can only repeat George Bernard Shaw's famous comment, 'It is enough that there is a beyond.' The movement has definitely lost steam. We are merely surviving with our backs to the wall. Not finding enough inspiration to do anything serious. I think only really sensitive people will be able to come out of it and shape the future.

Dipankar: You just mentioned your socio-political beliefs. You are also recognized as the father-figure of our political cinema. What are your thoughts on this?

Mrinal-da: But I have also heard that there is no political cinema in India. I am a bit confused on this issue, I do not think that political cinema is supposed to topple the government or make people indulge in sabotage. But what you say is also right, all my films have strong socio-political overtones, this trend started with me. Perhaps it was deliberate because I felt the need to express my political reaction to certain issues through my cinema. In the post-*Bhuvan Shome* period, the air of Calcutta was heavy with the smell of gunpowder, I could not avoid or ignore that. If at that time I expressed my political thoughts a bit bluntly, I don't think that is a crime.

Dipankar: There was an allegation that your cinema was nothing but political pamphlets.

Mrinal-da: I accept that. But if I can project a viewpoint artistically, what is wrong with that?

Dipankar: At that time, you used to claim that your aim was to provoke your audience.

Mrinal-da: Every artist does that. Even Tagore did.

Dipankar: But then you yourself abandoned that platform and returned to non-political cinema.

Mrinal-da: I really don't know what is political and what is non-political cinema. Wise critics will probably soon start talking about political novels and political painting. I admit that in the early seventies, I was a bit naïve; I thought revolution was knocking at the door. But I soon realized that I was wrong, and I required a little introspection. Since then, I have been trying to go deeper inside but it is an entirely political process. I still remember at the Bangalore International Film Festival in 1980 somebody asked the Cuban film-maker Tomas Alea in the press meet, 'Can you suggest a model political film?' He replied, 'Look at Mrinal Sen's film.' But there was no political overtone in that film!

Dipankar: Which film was that?

Mrinal-da: *Ek Din Pratidin*.

Dipankar: Ah! Now I remember, there were lots of controversies.

Mrinal-da: I have faced questions such as, 'What happened to your famous anger? That anger which broke glass panes and disrobed a mannequin? Now only smoke came out of the coal stove and the film ended.'

I have tried to reason with these critics—'Why do you go by the external manifestations? Please try to understand the innermost feelings, the feelings that make us dream'. In that sense, *Ek Din Pratidin* is to me a fully political film. You see, these days I do not shout from the rooftops; I now have the liberty, but I don't need to express myself loudly like that anymore.

Dipankar: Thank you, Mrinal-da, for this sweet confession, but can we, for some time, go back to the seventies when you used to shout from the rooftops? Through your Calcutta trilogy did you just want to capture the mood of the city, or did you have another idea, perhaps a need to express your political beliefs?

Mrinal-da: Although it is known as the Calcutta trilogy, those three films—*Interview*, *Calcutta 71*, *Padatik*—could have been shot in any third-world city—at least, that is what many film-makers from those countries have told me. I never tried to limit myself within the city limits. In these films, I have shown footage from Solanus' movie, clippings of the Vietnam War, the famine of Africa, etc. I have also talked about the Bangladesh Liberation War, although I could not procure any footage because my source on the other side of the border himself became a martyr.

Dipankar: Would it be right if I conclude that while shooting the trilogy, you thought about the globalization of cinema?

Mrinal-da: I have always thought in those terms. Didn't I tell you once that I feel I am a citizen of the world?

Dipankar: Yes, I remember.

Mrinal-da: What makes me sick is all this conversation I am hearing about our Indianness, our aggressive nationalism, how deep our roots are, etc. When my parents are Indian, I am automatically an Indian, what is there to talk about? It is like Romeo's remarks to the physician—'Show me where is Juliet in my body, I would chop that limb off.' Our culture is like that, you cannot make a physical display of that. Particularly in today's world where there is a constant fusion of various cultures. May I give you a true-life example?

Dipankar: Yes, please.

Mrinal-da: Many years ago, when my son was about five or six, I took him to a park in the afternoon. It was summer, the sky was overcast with dark clouds, a thunderstorm was brewing. Suddenly, there was a cloudburst with thunder and lightning, the entire sky lit up. My son cried with excitement, 'Look up! The sky looks like a 70-mm screen!' Just a week back we had taken him to see a film on a 70-mm screen, a unique experience for both father and son. If my father or grandfather had had a similar experience at the age of six, they probably would have exclaimed, 'Look up! Garuda is spreading his wings!' But my son has been born in an era when science and technology have unified the whole world. Living in this era, you have to be conscious of the extended world and at the same time learn how you can still remain an Indian.

Dipankar: Back to cinema again. After the trilogy, you made two films—entirely rural location, rural sentiments—*Mrigayaa* and *Oka Oori Katha*. But from *Parashuram* onwards, you have remained firmly Calcutta-centric. Your camera might have moved to the village in *Akaler Sandhane* and *Khandhar*, but the characters, the mood, is totally urban.

Mrinal-da: You are right. After *Parashuram* I felt that I could no longer make village-based films because I had become an outsider. Not me alone but our poets, writers and other creative people, we have all become foreigners. Although 75 per cent of my audience and readers are rural, our style of speaking and writing is 100 per cent urban.

Dipankar: That has been our trend in all art forms for quite some time. Did you not realize this before?

Mrinal-da: No, I had the mistaken notion that I understood the village and its people. It struck me much later that I was watching the village through an urban eye, like my creation, the great Mr Bhuvan Shome of the Indian Railways Service. In that film, the camera merely follows him, whatever he is watching and thinking are reflected on the screen. There is no difference between him and me. It is the same situation in *Akaler Sandhane*. I am now of the opinion that it is extremely difficult for a city-bred film-maker like me to truly portray rural life.

Dipankar: Is this only your problem or does a writer also suffer a similar handicap?

Mrinal-da: Since I am not a writer myself, I have to refer to Premchand, as in my opinion, there is no better chronicler of rural India than him. I did not know him personally, but his son has told me that his father never used any local lingo or dialect; his characters spoke in chaste Hindi because he felt that mixing up languages created hurdles for the readers.

Dipankar: He is right. For the general reader, it is a problem.

Mrinal-da: But the basic truth is that when even a great writer like Premchand writes about the poorest of the poor, his writing never reaches the target audience, in his mind he is writing for the urban middle class. That is why our writers do not feel the urge to become familiar with the intricacies of rural life. So only their lifestyle, which you can see with a few cosmetic visits to the villages, only that is reflected in their work. In the process they have to depend on a few token words, some topicalities of the dialects and some other such tricks and feel satisfied with their portrayal of rural life. Not only writers, but even our intellectuals have no respect for the lifestyle of the non-privileged. I know this from my own experience.

Dipankar: Can you elaborate upon your point?

Mrinal-da: You know I made *Mrigayaa*, which is based on the life of a tribal community, the Santhals. Before starting the film, I approached the head of the Anthropological Survey of India, a renowned scholar. I told him, 'I want to get in touch with somebody who knows the lifestyle of the Santhals.' He referred me to one of his students, who had done a doctorate on the Santhals and had spent seventeen years in the area where I was shooting.

I met that gentleman and asked him, 'Can you tell me whether the Santhals clap when they are happy?'

He remained silent for some time and then replied, 'I am a social anthropologist, this is not my subject, you better ask a physical anthropologist.'

Can you beat that? And this man claimed that he had spent seventeen years with the Santhals! I have not heard anything more stupid in my life!

Dipankar: But *Mrigayaa* is an outstanding film.

Mrinal-da: After that experience, though I completed *Mrigayaa*, I chose to return to city life. Since you were talking about my trilogy, let me mention that I made another trilogy in the next decade.

Dipankar: Another trilogy?

Mrinal-da: Let us take *Ek Din Pratidin*, made in 1979. In this film, a young girl, the only earning member of a family, suddenly does not return home one night. She is absent for most of the film, although the story is centred on her. The second film of the trilogy is *Kharij*, made in 1982. At the very beginning, the boy-servant of a family dies of carbon monoxide poisoning. He is not seen at all, although he dominates the movie. The third film is *Ek Din Achanak* of 1989, when the head of the family, a retired professor of history, suddenly leaves his home without any quarrel or altercation with his family members, and till the end of the movie, we do not know what happened to him.

These three films, made over one decade, are totally different from each other, yet a practising psychiatrist of London, Dr Somnath Zutshi, found a common factor in these films—in all these movies, the central figure is missing. He has named it 'the Absent Trilogy'. Whether you like it or not, it is an interesting theory and a totally different kind of analysis.

Dipankar: I never thought about it in that manner. But I found *Ek Din Achanak* to be highly autobiographical, as if you were going through a merciless self-analysis.

Mrinal-da: Strange! That is exactly what somebody told me after watching it at the Venice International Film Festival. My response was, 'You will hear the sound of my breath in every frame, but I am not sure whether it is autobiographical'. *Ek Din Achanak* has many sequences that are fragments of what actually happened in my life. But life is much more fascinating than fiction or film. Think about the letters I wrote to Gita during the making of *Akaler Sandhane*.

Dipankar: With regard to your experiences and experiments in film-making, will you tell us about *Genesis*? Not many Indian film-makers have gone through what you did.

Mrinal-da: You are right, because not many film-makers have made films jointly produced by a foreign government. *Genesis* could be made because of a cultural exchange programme between India and France. Subsequently, two other countries—Belgium and Switzerland—also joined the programme. The driving force behind the programme was my old friend and the then culture minister of France, M. Jack Lang. I asked Jack if it would be possible to make the film in any Indian language. He replied that it would require Presidential assent.

So, I called on President Mitterrand and made the same request.

He asked me, 'What is your language of preference?'

I said, 'Hindi.'

He said, 'Fine, no problem.'

He also gave me some other concessions.

Dipankar: Such as?

Mrinal-da: Generally, in the case of a foreign joint production, certain conventions are observed. For example, shooting is done in both countries and actors of both countries have to be included in the cast. But I got exemptions on both those counts. My film was shot entirely in India with an Indian cast. But the technical crew was all foreign. My cameraman was French, the sound recordist was from Belgium and the editor was Swiss. All over Europe, film crews observe a five-day week and work eight hours per day. For me, they worked all seven days and sometimes shifts stretched to fourteen hours. But no one complained. That is why the film was ready in record time.

Dipankar: But nobody in India got a chance to see the film!

Mrinal-da: What could I do? My Indian partner let me down and disappeared. The duplicate negative was with him, so I could not make a print.

Dipankar: Where is the master negative?

Mrinal-da: In France. The film was released in seven theatres. This is the somewhat sad story of *Genesis*. A great opportunity for me but a disappointment that my own people never got to see it.

Dipankar: Are you happy with the film?

Mrinal-da: Very broadly, yes, I am. But I would be happier to do it again. It is like my life, like my protagonist in *Ek Din Achanak*, I would love to have a second innings.

Dipankar: This is your philosophy of life. I am more interested in your aesthetic perceptions. Mrinal-da, is your cinema changing? As you hinted, are you becoming more introspective and delving deeper into life?

Mrinal-da: Yes, I am. I am no longer bothered about plot or incidents. I try to think about the feelings of my characters and make the film around that. When I joined this profession, our seniors taught me that cinema should be a string of events. From one event to another—that was how an ideal script should flow. But somehow, I am losing faith in this formula. I think the time has come to try something new in Indian cinema. It seems somebody has drawn a Lakshman rekha, but you must see what lies beyond. The language of cinema has become hackneyed, that also deserves a change. I would love to be the instrument of these changes, if possible, from my next film. I can see the smile on your face. You must be thinking that the old man is daydreaming and talking rubbish. But I really wish I could do it.

Dipankar: Mrinal-da, I am smiling because you just gave me a scoop, you talked about your new film. When do you plan to start, Mrinal-da?

Mrinal-da: Maybe tomorrow, maybe after a few years. Although I try to act smart, I am fully conscious of my age and advancing years and failing health. Sometimes, I think, have I forgotten how to think? But then I find myself reacting to happenings around me and coming out with bold reactions. Then I begin to ponder, if I can react so boldly, come up with statements that surprise people, why can't I design a new language for cinema? It is taking time, but it will come. I need a spark…

Dipankar: You have thoughts, some ideas, don't you?

Mrinal-da: Of course. Every morning, when I wake up, I think today is the day it will happen. In the course of the last few years, I have drafted innumerable scripts. Mind you, only rough drafts, nothing complete, but at least I know where I stand. Fifty years ago, when I threw my lot in with film-making, I had nothing before me, just like now. I only hoped something would happen, and it did happen. Maybe it will happen this time also.

Dipankar: We know from the media that you are still very sensitive to your environment. Your reaction to our nuclear experiment at Pokhran was not universally appreciated, but it revealed your thoughts.

Mrinal-da: Thank you, but this is something I want to clarify. I have visited Hiroshima and have seen what happened there. I am not an emotional or sentimental person, but what I saw brought tears to my eyes; there was absolutely no need for the bombing. By that time the war was practically over, and it was clear who the winner was. Yet the bomb was dropped on Hiroshima on 6 August and on Nagasaki three days later. I want the entire world to ban nuclear weapons.

Dipankar: I have finally reached this journey's end. I have just one more question before I drop the curtain. While you have been seeking a new language for cinema, you have also been playing a special role for some time. You are now an Honourable Member of Parliament. Please tell us something about this role.

Mrinal-da: Some time ago, His Excellency the President of India nominated me to the Rajya Sabha. It was an honour, so I did not refuse, but I don't think it was a very wise decision because such things do not go with my character. Now I come to Delhi for every session at least for a few days, and when I am in Parliament, I attend the Question Hour regularly just to watch the discomfort of our mighty ministers before the sharp arrows from the Opposition benches. But my curiosity ends there.

During my early days, I had asked one senior member, 'Listen, I am going to be non-collegiate occasionally, but how many classes do I have to attend to avoid being discollegiate?'

He assured me, 'Do not worry. Even if you bunk a whole session, your percentage will be protected.'

So, I come here at the start of each session for three or four days then go back to Calcutta. Sometimes I return for a few days before the close of the session. Some days ago, one member jokingly told me, 'You drop in here like the intruders in Kashmir and also disappear like them.'

I told him, 'Do not underestimate intruders. Decades ago, one such intruder gatecrashed Indian cinema and changed its contours. His name was Satyajit Ray. Maybe one day I will do something revolutionary here. One never knows. The future is always shrouded in mystery.'

Dipankar: Thank you, Mrinal-da. Take care. We will resume our dialogue once you find the new language of film or the will to shoot another film.

Mrinal-da: Thank you. I don't know when that will happen, if it will happen at all. But come again soon.

*

This is where I switched off the recorder and we brought our talkathon to a close. I was the listener who dared to provoke and Mrinal-da, the maverick maestro, enjoyed recounting his experiences, his thoughts. Our conversation was spread over eight months in different locales in Delhi and Calcutta. My estimate is that the total duration of recording was over ten hours. I think this is the longest interview the maestro ever gave in his six-decade-long career. What is amazing is that despite his age (he was over seventy-six when we started), he enjoyed every moment of the talking, did not feel tired, and his memory was amazingly sharp with details. I must also mention Gita Boudi, who supported him in this recounting, filling in interesting details and titbits. And, in spite of his early mandatory warning, Mrinal Sen never contradicted himself.

5

The Last Word

Fourteen days before Mrinal Sen was born in Faridpur, in what is now Bangladesh, India celebrated its first Labour Day. On 1 May 1923, communist leader Malayapuram Singaravelu Chettiar raised, for the first time, the red flag that would become an emblem of communism in India. This is the sort of quirky coincidence that you'd expect in a novel—that the film-maker whose work was so deeply informed by Marxist idealism would be born in the same year that May Day was celebrated for the first time in the country. It happened in Mrinal-da's life.

A hundred years later, Marxism has lost much of its shine, and the history of May Day is largely forgotten. What of Mrinal Sen? In the age of multiplex cinemas and superhero films, are his films relevant anymore? Does his belief in a certain kind of cinema and his disregard for commercial returns have any place in our contemporary culture?

Mrinal-da belonged to a generation of film-makers who joined the profession almost accidentally, but who persisted with it all the same. The movie business was full of risks and not considered particularly respectable. There was no film school or any training institute in the country, which meant all those interested were either self-taught or had gone abroad to receive training. Satyajit Ray is one of the few of his generation who was exposed to cinema from an early age. In contrast, Mrinal Sen was not much of a moviegoer, and had it not been for the jobless days that led to him pottering around the National Library in Calcutta, he may have spent his life pottering about in college laboratories. Ritwik Ghatak, whose love for storytelling and performance began with theatre and jatra, once said, 'I joined cinema because through it, I could reach the masses. If I get another medium which would give me a bigger access, I would give cinema a big kick in the backside and join that media.'

In his time, Sen stood out for how startlingly modern he was. Inspired by the masters of Soviet cinema and the IPTA, he saw cinema as an instrument of social change and as an art form that could convince people to discard old ways. He had no patience for any of society's holy cows. For instance, he is a rare Bengali artist of the twentieth century in whose work Rabindranath Tagore has barely any presence. The only use of Rabindrasangeet that comes to my mind is in *Pratinidhi*, made at the beginning of his career, and in his last movie, *Aamar Bhuvan*. In fact, music played very little role in his films, which is unusual, particularly in Bengali cinema, even when made by parallel cinema directors. Can we ever forget how famous Ray and Ghatak are for the way they wove music into their films? When music did sneak into his stories, Sen used protest music, like *ganasangeet* (choral songs), associated with the IPTA, in *Chorus* and *Akaler Sandhane*.

Sen belongs to a generation that defined Indianness for a country that was newly independent and finding itself. If commercial cinema gave the country the comfort of happy endings and aspirational fantasies, Sen's films were truly a parallel cinema. They were rooted in lived experience and they put forward ideas that were radical at the time—that the everyday is also art, that there was more to being aesthetic than putting up images of conventional beauty. Sen's involvement and familiarity with the major socio-political developments in the subcontinent was the foundation for his films.

If you ask me what distinguishes Mrinal-da's cinema from that of others, it is his austerity. He has a filmography comprising twenty-eight feature films, four documentaries, one telefilm and a thirteen-episode tele-series. Of these, only one was made with the aim of making money and that is *Bhuvan Shome*, a pan-India super-hit long before that term had the aura it does today. Yet Mrinal-da never made a secret of having made *Bhuvan Shome* mostly out of consideration for a friend who needed money. In fact, not only did he repay the loan that was taken out to make the film, he even returned part of the sanctioned budget because it hadn't been utilized. In his crisp white cotton kurta pyjama, which became his lifelong uniform, he added dignity and elegance to austerity. He stood out as much for his six-foot-tall frame as he did for his integrity. There was never even a whiff of scandal about this man from Faridpur who became Calcutta's most loving chronicler. I often remember the question he asked Ray, 'Don't you feel lonely at times?' Because that was Mrinal-da's own experience, the loneliness of a long-distance runner. It is the aloofness that came from his commitment to a certain set of ideals and a certain kind of cinema that kept Sen on the fringes, despite all the prizes and acclaim he won in India and abroad. After all, there are contemporaries of his who have written voluminous memoirs, where he hardly figured.

So why is Mrinal Sen worth remembering? Is it because he is the first film-maker in India's arthouse cinema to have a pan-India hit? Or is it because he ushered in a new genre of film-making and introduced new styles of storytelling to Indian cinema? Both are true and good reasons for him to occupy pride of place in the annals of Indian and international cinema. He, like Ray, also introduced a galaxy of new talent to Bengali cinema. Here's a list of names off the top of my head:

1. Shubhendu Chatterjee (*Akash Kusum*, 1965)
2. Prashanta Nanda (*Matira Manisha*, 1966)
3. Suhasini Mulay (*Bhuvan Shome*, 1969)
4. Sadhu Meher (*Bhuvan Shome*, 1969)
5. Ranjit Mallick (*Interview*, 1970)
6. Vivek Chatterjee (*Ek Adhuri Kahani*, 1971)
7. Mithun Chakraborty (*Mrigayaa*, 1976)
8. Mamata Shankar (*Mrigayaa*, 1976)
9. Sreela Majumdar (*Parashuram*, 1978)
10. Arun Mukhopadhyay (*Parashuram*, 1978)

11. Kaushik Sen (*Ek Din Pratidin*, 1979)
12. Anjan Dutt (*Chaalchitra*, 1981)
13. Anasuya Majumdar (*Mahaprithibi*, 1991)

In addition to this, Kanika Majumdar, famous for Ray's *Teen Kanya*, made her debut in *Punshcha* (but the film took time to be completed). Madhabi Mukherjee's first film was Tapan Sinha's *Tonsil*, but her brilliance as an actor came out only in her second film, *Baishey Shravana*.

However, ultimately an artist is remembered not as a collection of data points but for what their art evokes in audiences. At first glance, Sen's cinema seems rooted in the past. The times are gone and the New Wave that he pioneered has been relegated to history. The lived experiences of the middle class that he loved to show on the big screen are today frequently packaged in gloss, glamour and consumerism. And yet, cinema of protest remains, and the emotional intensity of Sen's films is unmistakable. The trappings of modernity may have changed, but the dilemmas, the crises, the hypocrisies and the heartbreaks remain strangely constant. We go back to the films of greats like Sen, Ray and Ghatak because they make us see the world around us differently. They leave us richer and fuller with every film because these greats were seeking truth through their stories.

Mrinal Sen's cinema deserves to be celebrated and remembered because of the time that it captures, but it is also true that his films continue to feel relatable despite being from a bygone era. While the contexts are time- and space-specific, the emotions they tap into remain true for contemporary India. So long as there are people made invisible by others, so long as one social class can exploit another, so long as there are silent screams, Mrinal Sen and his cinema of protest will remain.